Mary's Story

Hope Revealed

By Mary Bulthuis

---

with Bill Koch

For Erin, Ellen, Kevin and Brian

In memory of
David

MARY'S STORY 🍃 HOPE REVEALED
Mary Bulthuis with Bill Koch
Copyright © 2010 by Mary Bulthuis and Bill Koch

Proforma Lakeshore Print & Promotions
PO Box 1392
Frankfort, IL 60423
815-534-5461
815-534-5462 (fax)

Find us on the Web at: www.hope-revealed.com

Editor: Bill Koch
Cover design: Bill Koch
Photos: Mary Bulthuis
Interior design and layout: Bill Koch

ISBN 13: 978-0-615-39698-9

ISBN 10: 0615396984

Printed and bound in the United States of America

Acknowledgement

They say that one of the reasons marriage is good is that we have a witness to our lives. As my marriage fell apart 25 years ago, I began writing – and the *pen and paper* became my witness.

I tried to put these writings together in a book form many times without success. In 2008, after watching the movie *The Bucket List* with my husband, I told him I had always wanted to write a book and I promised to work on it. A few months later, a neighbor and his wife walked closely with me through the most devastating loss of my life. After this loss, I approached this neighbor, Bill Koch, to help me create this book.

I thank God for Bill and the gifts God has given him to make it possible for me to fulfill this promise. This is a book that tells the story God has written in my life. I am sharing it in the hope that it will give someone else hope. I pray you receive it. Jesus Christ died and purchased hope for all of us. This hope has sustained me through my darkest hours.

HOPE REVEALED

Table of Contents

Foreword

> FOR WE ARE GOD'S WORKMANSHIP, CREATED IN CHRIST JESUS
> TO DO GOOD WORKS, WHICH GOD PREPARED IN ADVANCE
> FOR US TO DO. — EPHESIANS 2:10

We were all created by God's workmanship to do good works. God prepared a book in advance for me to do and I am finally being obedient. It took denying many negative voices to push through to finish what you have in your hands. I believe my story is unique, because God created us each so uniquely. I believe God loves us so much that He wants us to share this Love, which includes Hope, with others.

Jesus Christ finished the work on the Cross and has Hope to reveal in your life, too. He died to save us and give us life abundantly.

I pray you enjoy this story, but I pray you also enjoy your story – whatever you are facing. God loves you and is waiting to save you from anything that is not bringing joy into your life. He can do it right now – today – right where you are. *Hope Revealed!*

For Jesus' Glory.

ONE

An Already Full Family

Is it possible that when you have six daughters and one son and are in the delivery room hearing "It's a girl!" you may think – I've run out of girls' names?!? Because, when they brought me home from the hospital, I didn't have a name. I was simply the eighth child born to my parents. My birth certificate, to this day, has no first or second name; just a last name, the date of birth and my parents' names. That is my identification. I was the eighth child born into an already full family. Four more were to follow – two more girls and two more boys – a dozen children in all.

Do we all think everyone else lives like we do as children? It wasn't until I was 12 that I realized our family was considered poor compared to many others. Being raised with 12 children, day old doughnuts given for free by the baker and hand me down clothes from other families seemed normal to me. Standing in line to use the bathroom every morning was normal, in a three bedroom, one bath home. Waiting in line to get your hair braided. Walking around the block with the big, black, baby buggy, rocking your younger siblings. Playing kick-the-can out front on the street until dark. Fielding our own baseball team on long summer days. This was all normal in our family growing up in Northlake. My grandparents, in Chicago, moved us out of their basement to a home in the suburbs with open fields for all of us children to play in. It wasn't until I was 12 and got my first paycheck from the grocer that I realized I could eat two Twinkies - the entire package - if I wanted to! Before that paycheck, I remember nothing but sharing and waiting in lines.

Somehow, our parents kept us in Catholic school even though we didn't have the money for hot lunch, when it was offered. Dad had a gambling issue and mom struggled to keep our heads above water – it was a constant battle to make ends meet with little money and lots of mouths to feed.

At school, we were taught by stern nuns who hadn't quite learned all the Biblical principles. A few of them were kind, but the majority implied we were doing something wrong. I feared them, yet wanted to become one. Mom said I had to wait until after high school to go to "nun school."

Who wouldn't want a nun's lifestyle? It seemed like such a wonderful existence. The convent was a quiet, calm place, as I found out when I worked there one summer – until I spilled my milkshake on the rug. Meals were organized and there was enough food for everyone. At my home, if you were slow to fill your plate, too bad. There were no seconds and not always quite enough *firsts*. Also, I never liked worrying about what clothes I had to wear. If I became a nun, my clothes would already be picked out for me. Even better, I would match all of the other nuns - no comparisons!

I pictured my evenings as a nun reading quietly or praying. It seemed to me like a perfect life. A nun picked Jesus for a husband. I remember looking at their wedding ring finger and knowing the ring they wore meant they were married to Jesus. Wow! What better husband was there? It was the life I wanted.

The nuns were my teachers and I tried hard to please them. Some of them couldn't be pleased. Mother Perpetua was a principal that grabbed children by their cheeks, lifted them off the ground and shook them. You could always tell if someone had been to the principal's office by the red face they walked around with. Fear of her kept many children in line and I was no exception.

I worked hard at obeying. When Sister Mark left the room in fifth grade and all the children started flinging rubber bands at each other, many landed on my desk. I held one in my hand for a long time, turning it over and over – enjoying the elasticity – and being entertained by examining it. After watching hundreds of rubber bands fly across the room, I finally did aim one at a friend. It was a direct hit. The room was filled with laughter, an unusual sound in our classroom.

When Sister returned, she was aghast at the site of hundreds of rubber bands covering the classroom like a beige blanket. She looked around and then asked everyone who even shot one rubber band to raise his or her hand. I had shot one. Literally one. So, I raised my hand. Robert raised his too.

We were the only two! Now, really, could anyone have believed that two children shot that many rubber bands?!?

It didn't matter what she believed.

We were both given a four-stanza poem to memorize that night. For me, it was a poem adapted from Rudyard Kipling's poem *If*, but it's verses were adapted to give a special meaning to girls. I had to recite it the next morning at a podium with a microphone. I still remember it to this day because I stayed in my bedroom all night committing it to memory.

If you can hear the whispering about you
And never yield to deal in whispers, too;
If you can bravely smile when loved ones doubt you
And never doubt, in turn, what loved ones do;
If you can keep a sweet and gentle spirit
In spite of fame or fortune, rank or place,
And though you win your goal or only near it,
Can win with poise or lose with equal grace;

If you can meet with unbelief, believing,
And hallow in your heart, a simple creed,
If you can meet Deception, undeceiving,
And learn to look to God for all you need;
If you can be what girls should be to mothers:
Chums in joy and comrades in distress,
And be unto others as you'd have the others
Be unto you – no more, and yet no less;

If you can keep within your heart the power
To say that firm, unconquerable "No,"
If you can brave a present shadowed hour
Rather than yield to build a future woe;
If you can love, yet not let loving master,
But keep yourself within your own self's clasp,
And not let Dreaming lead you to disaster
Nor Pity's fascination loose your grasp;

If you can lock your heart on confidences
Nor ever needlessly in turn confide;
If you can put behind you all pretenses
Of mock humility or foolish pride;
If you can keep the simple, homely virtue
Of walking right with God – then have no fear
That anything in all the world can hurt you –
And – which is more – you'll be a Woman, dear.

It was worth memorizing, but the punishment didn't seem fair. It was, however, noticed.

In sixth grade, when Robert and I won the prestigious John F. Kennedy Catholic Youth Award, I was thrilled. It took me years to connect our honesty with the rubber bands to that award – given to one sixth grade girl and one sixth grade boy.

Then came a Friday in early September of 1964.

I was sitting in the living room watching dad puff upward with his mouth. Mom screamed and made us all leave the house. We went next door and as we saw the priest coming up the stairs an hour later, we knew dad was gone. He had suffered several heart attacks before and was not expected to live a long life.

Life changed a lot for all of us when mom had to work full-time. Even though dad didn't bring home a lot of his paycheck because he gambled, it was different with mom working now. Her days were spent as a checker at a grocery store and nights as a waitress at a cocktail club. We had to do more chores, including cooking for each other and especially raising the younger ones.

Mom said we couldn't go back to our school but the priests made it possible. The nuns bought us shoes. What embarrassing shoes we wore – black, squeaky nun shoes – in the midst of junior high. Not a good way to fit in with peers.

Even though I mostly played with other Catholic kids, my next-door neighbor and best friend went to the public school. Her family had a lot of problems as her dad was often drunk. She physically attacked me one day, telling me I needed to learn how to fight in case my Mom needed to send me to the public school. She also used the "F" word and said my parents had to do it 12 times to have 12 children. I argued with her that my parents never did that. My Mom asked me about it later that evening, so I guess the mom's talked about our argument.

My mom wasn't too skilled in talking about life or body issues. She tried to talk to me about becoming a woman once and when I asked one question she immediately shook her head and left the room. That didn't prompt any future discussion, so I quizzed my peers with my anatomy questions.

My sisters danced a lot and taught us how to dance. The jitterbug was a big hit in our living room. Bill, a neighbor next door with a dog named Bingo, taught square dance lessons on Friday evenings in his basement. With such a large family, we only needed a few friends and could rustle up eight or 12 people pretty quickly – "Allemande Left With The Old Left Hand."

Those were fun Friday evenings. If I close my eyes, I can still hear that square dance music coming out of his basement window on a hot summer night as I drifted off to sleep. Of course, drifted is a unique word to use for trying to fall asleep in a bed with four siblings poking you in the side.

I loved dancing growing up and my older sister became a pom-pom girl and taught us younger siblings the routines. We often performed a routine to Herb Alpert's *Whipped Cream* for any of my parents' friends or other relatives. Once I got to high school, it was easy to try out and make the squad.

Just before high school, I remember going to a dance in eighth grade with Joe. The day after the dance, my older sister asked me what I had done last night and I told her I had danced.

"I talked to Gail, Joe's older sister and she said that he said you looked ridiculous and he couldn't figure out what you were doing."

UGH! How awful. I thought I danced and my partner didn't know what I was doing. This experience became a huge burden for me!

It wasn't until 20 years later that I decided not to care what others were thinking about how I danced. They didn't need to notice or watch me. I was going to have fun on the dance floor and enjoy the music.

Music is so uplifting. It may be one of my great escapes and great comforts. When I sing, I put myself in the song. When Bobby Rydel sang to Ann Margaret in *Bye Bye Birdie*, I was Ann Margaret and he was singing to me. When Tammy was in love singing to the doctor, I was in love and would sing the song over and over. I memorized the sound track to *Funny Girl* as a teenager because I sympathized with Fannie Brice.

Tammy

I hear the cottonwoods whisp'rin' above
Tammy! Tammy! Tammy's in love!
The ole hootie owl hootie-hoo's to the dove
Tammy! Tammy! Tammy's in love!
Does my lover feel what I feel
When he comes near?
My heart beats so joyfully
You'd think that he could hear!
Wish I knew if he knew what I'm dreaming of!
Tammy! Tammy! Tammy's in love! [1]

I realize it was a bit of a fantasy world, but music had always provided an outlet of a wonderful life and I chose songs that ministered to me.

Mom remarried five years after dad passed. We only met Mike once, but trusted mom. We moved into his home with his four children, so sixteen children in all, but some were married by then. Life became a little more normal because mom was able to stay home and cook. And, we liked Mike.

College was not an option for the girls in our family. We were raised to believe that girls were supposed to graduate from high school, marry and have children. My sister and I tried to go to junior college (I had hopes of becoming either a math teacher or psychologist), but the cost and time it took away from our full time jobs didn't allow us to finish.

❀

THERE IS SURELY A FUTURE HOPE FOR YOU, AND YOUR HOPE WILL NOT BE CUT OFF. — PROVERBS 23:18

TWO

Marry And Have Children

Working full time, I hung around with friends and met "him." We sat at a party, the only two sitting behind the bar in a friend's basement and talked. I was 18 and he was 20. We talked about our lives to that point, what we were willing to share, and by the end of the evening, I knew I wanted to know him better. When my friends asked him what he thought of me, he said I was a little overweight for him. I weighed 150 pounds. I decided to count calories and I lost 15 pounds over three months.

The next time I saw him, we talked again and, at 135 pounds, he was attracted to me. He continued to call and talk. I remember creating a poem about my feelings. I remember one particular line.

> *"We talked about marriage and having kids.*
> *Funny, but now I want mine to be his."*

He had a good heart and great expectations for children he might have some day. I decided he would make a great husband and dad.

His friends called him "cornball." He was very funny – always joyful and cracking jokes. His smile would light up a room and he was kind to everyone. It was easy to fall in love with him.

He did have some money problems, so on some dates I would drive. When the evening was over and we arrived at his home, he would get out of the car fast. I learned his dad had a drinking problem that he didn't want me to see. Whenever I saw his dad drunk, he just seemed happy to me.

In 1973, when I was 20, we married and I thought I had finally done something right. Remember, I believed girls were supposed to marry and have children. I was halfway there.

The first time I noticed something different about him was on our honeymoon. He got mad at me and called me stupid for the way I took a picture at Disney World. His demeanor changed in a flash. He had been smiling, then really angry, then smiling again.

Driving home from the airport, we were told his younger brother was hospitalized with a bullet wound – he had been shot while we were away on our honeymoon. I tried to hug him to say I was sorry and he pulled away. Married one week and I fell asleep crying because he pushed me away emotionally. I didn't understand why he didn't want the offer of my comfort.

Every once in a while he would talk disrespectfully to his mother. And, sometimes he would talk of hating his father for his drinking. I didn't understand, because during our courtship, his father seemed so nice to me and my husband seemed so polite to his parents. His best friend had a wife I knew and she told me about his abuse. She mentioned that he would come to school all black and blue – all beaten up. In those days, you didn't talk about things like that. So, it seemed to me that the abuse had time to fester in him and contributed to his hidden anger that surfaced now and then.

A few months into our marriage, I was told I was pregnant. How exciting! I became a mother on December 30, 1974 – I was going to make it – married and the mother of a beautiful daughter, Erin. It didn't get any better than that! God sent us a second daughter Ellen in 1976, a son Kevin in 1979 and a second son Brian in 1981. We were blessed with four beautiful children.

He was the man I thought I married most of the time for the first several years. He was a good father at the beginning and had fun with our daughters. By the time our sons were born, his drinking problem and his demons had increased immensely and he was too involved in his pain to have anything to give to me or any of the children. There was no reason for us to have any respect or love of any kind for him as a parent – he wasn't able to parent. He was wounded and controlled by demons of anger and addiction.

On the outside, we looked like a beautiful family, because he never showed his *other* side in public. Only in our home at night. He was unable to hold any job, unable to stay away from the pull of alcohol to numb his pain, unable to love, parent or support his family. Any semblance of family life deteriorated quickly.

One evening, his friends were over for a barbeque and I went downstairs to see how the children were playing. In a large basement playroom, on a table alongside the pages I typed for court reporters (trying to earn money while staying home with the children) was a large white pile of cocaine. The men standing there were shocked to see me. I asked them to leave as I cleared the area of my work papers. I went panicky inside and quickly moved the children out of the room. One of the three apologized to me. He agreed that it shouldn't have been around the children – shouldn't have been in my home. I started shaking inside. The feeling came over me that my life was not only out of control, but I felt forced into a very unpleasant place. I was fearful that something illegal was going on in my home – around my children – and possibly endangering them and me. Could I be considered an accomplice in a drug deal and go to jail? Who would raise my children?

During the next few years, I met some friends who tried to take him to Alcoholics Anonymous and I attended Al-Anon. His anger increased for suggesting he had a drinking problem and I stopped attending when he set fire to my 12-step books in the kitchen.

I read books about drinking and abusive behavior and learned a lot. This knowledge helped me look for more avenues of help for him and my marriage, but as I tried to understand more, he seemed to resent me more. He hated my faith and mocked me every time I mentioned God or church. He never attended.

He had endangered my life so many times that we eventually stopped going out as a couple. He would not let me drive home when he had been drinking and he would drive like a maniac – ignore stoplights – actually any laws – after a few drinks. At family bowling parties, weddings or gatherings of friends, he would get drunk and not let me drive home. He would run red lights and laugh at my fearful face. He would stop the car anywhere, get out and shout obscenities to anyone. He would "egg" a home or business. I would try to get the keys but the battle seemed worse than the thought of the car crash. On the way

Go Your Own Way
Loving you
Isn't the right thing to do
How can I ever change things
That I feel

If I could
Maybe I'd give you my world
How can I
When you won't take it from me

You can go your own way
Go your own way
You can call it
Another lonely day
You can go your own way
Go your own way [2]

home from a wedding one night, I was so scared I would die because of his reckless driving and not be able to raise my children, I vowed to never get in a car with him again.

One evening in late fall, he had a strange look in his eyes. As I tried to talk to him, he ran out of our home with only his socks on. As he ran down the block, I called a baby sitter and when she arrived, I ran after him. I had called an ambulance and they arrived as I tried to walk him back toward our home. Hallucinating, he said he was the devil.

The ambulance ride was scary – as I faced him I noticed his eyes looked very weird. The hospital admitted him because of his irrational behavior in the emergency room. After testing, he was told his liver was damaged from too much alcohol and the hallucinations were probably caused by breathing in too many paint fumes. He promised to stop drinking. He agreed to see a priest for counseling. We went to one session where he told the priest he wouldn't drink or use drugs anymore. I left that meeting hopeful.

A few days later, standing over the crib at home, I heard his friend arrive. Within minutes, the two of them were sharing a joint. The little hope I had for his recovery vanished.

Most days, it was easier not to think about how awful my life had become and just hope it would get better someday. Hope that somehow he would change and begin being a husband and dad.

It never did get better. In fact, it continued to get worse.

→ ψ ←

WHY ARE YOU DOWNCAST, O MY SOUL? WHY SO DISTURBED WITHIN ME? PUT OUR HOPE IN GOD, FOR I WILL YET PRAISE HIM, MY SAVIOR AND MY GOD. — PSALM 42:5

THREE

What Was God Thinking

I walked into the room and held her hand. I noticed her nail polish had grown out – Barb and I were alike in some ways as sisters – neither of us spent a lot of time on our nails. Her hand was limp as I laid it back down on the bed. We had been called on Saturday that she was hospitalized with a headache. We were called on Monday morning to go to the hospital to say goodbye. They called it a brain aneurism. Forty-two years old with six children – a really good person who held benefits to raise money for cancer research because our step-sister had died of cancer. I wondered - what was God thinking?

Several months later, Mike's cancer got the best of his body. Mike had been a good step-dad. My dad, Walt, had passed away when I was 11 and Mike became my stepdad when I was a teenager. He took me through some tough dating years. His ordination as a deacon in the Catholic Church at Holy Name Cathedral was a proud day for all of us. He loved God and we walked to mass at St. Charles many mornings throughout my high school years. He walked me down the aisle when I married and visited with bags of groceries when I was a young mom with an unemployed husband. When I rubbed his back to ease his pain during his last month, we didn't speak much. He had been my dad for 15 years and our love didn't need words.

Within the same year, my grandma passed away at the age of 93, and that seemed understandable. After all, life got pretty hard for her body. She had cancer in her 60s yet lived another 30 years. Her passing was easier to accept, but when I saw my mom collapse at her funeral, after losing a daughter – my sister, a husband – my stepdad, and a mother – my gram, in such a short time, mom crumbled. Along with her, something inside of me crumbled. My insides turned hard and cold.

I remember thinking, *if this is how you treat people who love you God, I don't want anything to do with you.*

You see, my mom loved God. We were raised to eat fish and cheese more than just during Lent and Advent. We were raised to kneel on hardwood floors, praying the rosary every First Friday of the month. We were raised to go to mass and Catholic School and we didn't speak on Good Friday between noon and 3:00 PM. After all, what was there to say while Jesus hung on the cross? And, this was her reward?? This tremendous pain was what she got from God??

I continued to take my children to church every week. They didn't notice the difference, but church and God meant nothing to me.

My marriage got harder, he drank more and more. Under the influence, he became a man I didn't know or want to be around. He had always been verbally abusive, saying he was kidding, but now he became mean and started pushing us around.

My life became a pit, a deep, cold, dark pit.

"I don't want to go inside," I said to my sister as she dropped me off one evening.

"What do you mean?" she asked.

"I really hate going into my home," I said.

"Hate going into your home?"

"You have no idea what it is like."

"Mary, you have children."

"Oh, it's not the children, I just can't live like I'm living anymore. I don't know how to put up with his behavior any longer."

"What do you mean, the drinking?"

"Oh, it is much more than his drinking now. It's gotten way out of hand. It's a horrible way to live."

"Listen to what you are saying – if it is a horrible way to live, why are you making four children live like that? Why aren't you doing something about it?"

"What am I going to do about it? I have four children and no money. We don't own a thing. He's never worked long enough for us to have a mortgage, a car that works, anything."

"Well, I don't have an answer, but I sure know there has to be some answer that's better than going into a home you can't stand to go into."

She said it with such confidence.

As I walked in that night, I realized there had to be an answer. I just didn't know it. My heart was heavy as I looked around and saw the unhappiness on my children's faces. He was asleep on the couch again. He always fell asleep if I stepped out. It was his way of showing me he wasn't going to watch the kids. So, I tucked them all in good night and hoped it would be a quiet evening.

On a usual night, I would fall asleep and then be woken up, anytime between 2:00 and 3:00 am, when the drinking would escalate to a level that made him uncontrollable. He would either be cooking something and there would be grease, eggs, milk and orange juice all over the kitchen or he would be watching TV and throwing things at the set because he didn't like what they were saying.

One night, he broke our clock that hung above the TV and as the glass shattered, I awoke. I went into the children's room, as I normally did, locked the door and slept between their bunks. I would get up in the morning and hope that he had gone off to work. Most times, he would still be in bed.

I would clean up the mess in the kitchen, make the children's breakfast and send them off to school. Then, I would clean up the bathroom. He would often vomit and miss the toilet.

One night, I was asleep and found myself on the floor. I climbed back to bed and was on the floor again. I realized he was pulling me off of the bed by my ankles. The third time I was thrown to the floor, pain shot up my back and I cried as I crawled out of the room into the children's bedroom. Thank God he shouted but didn't break through the kids' door and I fell asleep.

I was emotionally, physically and mentally broken. Every part of my heart, body, and mind cried out for any tiny drop of relief.

What happened to sanity? My life seemed like a bad dream and I wasn't waking up.

My hours became consumed with thinking of ways to try to keep him sober – consumed with thoughts of keeping him away from the children – consumed with cries to God for money to pay our bills – a God who I had decided I wanted nothing to do with.

Yet on some of the worst nights I would cry to the God I believed in as a child.

"God, life has gotten so hard. I don't know how to live like this any longer. Please help me, Father. I don't know if I want to wake up in the morning. It's not that I want to die, I just don't know if I can handle this life anymore."

✢ ☙ ✢

BUT THOSE WHO HOPE IN THE LORD WILL RENEW THEIR STRENGTH. THEY WILL SOAR ON WINGS LIKE EAGLES; THEY WILL RUN AND NOT GROW WEARY, THEY WILL WALK AND NOT BE FAINT. — ISAIAH 40:31

FOUR

Warm My Cold Heart

A friend invited me to a women's retreat at church in 1985. I went to take a break. I thought it would force him to parent if I was gone for the weekend. I was nervous for my children, but I had begun to learn about enabling at the Al-Anon meetings I had attended. He did agree I could go to church for the weekend, and this retreat was called *Christ Renews His Parish*.

When I went, they sat us down at small discussion tables and gave us a small Bible called *The Good News*. I remembered my Bible at home. I never remembered opening it, though. It was the prettiest book I owned, with a large, white puffy cover and crisp, gold pages. I think I had written my wedding date in it when I got it as a wedding present. I slowly inspected this small one, but put it on the table when the leader began asking us to open it and read the first words that hit our eyes. I listened to the other ladies at the table with indifference. When it came my turn, I gently spoke to the leader.

"I'll take a pass. This sounds like hocus-pocus to me."

She paused and glanced at my name tag.

"Humor me, Mary."

I waited. Okay, I came to this weekend, so I might as well play along with their games. As I grasped the soft cover book and opened it with each thumb, I read aloud from the page.

JESUS SAID TO HER, "MARY." SHE TURNED TOWARD HIM AND CRIED OUT IN ARAMAIC, "RABBONI!" (WHICH MEANS TEACHER). — JOHN 20:16

As the words were leaving my mouth, I grasped what I was saying and immediately put the book back on the table. The ladies waited.

"I don't care if He calls me by name, I don't want anything to do with Him."

Throughout the weekend, with the songs, love shown, talks and Scripture readings, something inside me began to melt.

The love of Christ, through these women, on this weekend, began to warm my cold heart. My emotions, my physical state, my feelings and my mind started to feel warmth again. Whatever had been cold inside of me for a long time basked in their presence – as if I were lying on a lawn chair on a beach basking in the sweet rays of the sun. I actually laughed, began to experience the love of others again and then surrendered. I surrendered my life to Christ and asked Him to take control of it – to become my personal Savior. He had control anyway, but I was under the illusion that I had to control things and had lost control. He broke through my illusion. I accepted the truth that I was loved by God, was His child and He had a plan for my life. Even though it wasn't the plan I thought he should have had for my life. I emptied myself by surrendering and it felt good to give over my illusion of control.

One woman on the retreat was always smiling. She had the

happiest attitude. I asked about her and they told me that she had lost two sons to cancer over the past few years. Both of her sons were young fathers who had died in her arms. I was shocked, so I made it a point to speak to her. She told me that it isn't God that we should get mad at when our lives are painful – God is there to help us through the tough times. This world is full of pain and the god of this world, satan, is who we need to get mad at. God controls and directs our lives and does have a plan that will end up for His glory but we first have to get through this world's garbage with His help.

I went home renewed and alive. As I walked into my home, I realized that I had changed, but my surroundings had not.

With Jesus as the Lord of my life, my life didn't get easier right away. In fact, some of my most difficult years were to follow. My husband had always been negative and angry, but then he became verbally abusive, began spanking the children more than necessary and started pushing us around a little. He even resorted to kicking our dog. I didn't connect all of this to physical abuse at the time, but I now understand these were signs of other things to come.

Fortunately, I had the Holy Spirit to guide me, women to pray for me – women to stand by me and look things up in the Bible to find answers. These women encouraged me and showed me how much God loves me. When things got rough, I clung to Scripture. I remember the first verse I memorized.

"FOR I KNOW THE PLANS I HAVE FOR YOU," DECLARES THE LORD, "PLANS TO PROSPER YOU AND NOT TO HARM YOU, PLANS TO GIVE YOU HOPE AND A FUTURE." — JEREMIAH 29:11

For now, I had to live in my home as best as I could. I made the best of a difficult lifestyle for about another year and a half. He would lose more jobs. Of course, not arriving for work in the morning as a result of all night drinking can cause a problem with employers. There was no food in the fridge and the money I got from watching other children quickly depleted. I got tired of being hungry and watching my children have sad faces. I slowly moved through each day hoping and praying that he would change. Any of my suggestions were met with sarcasm and laughter. I finally decided someone had to work full time for our children to eat regularly.

My girlfriend Donna and I coached our daughters' baseball team together and she was a good ear during those difficult years.

"I don't know how much longer I can live like I am, Donna, with no money for food. I think I should go to work full time," I said one day at one of our practices.

"My husband is looking for a secretary," she said, matter of fact. Her husband was the mayor of our small town of 8,000.

I had been a secretary, but that was so many years before. We discussed the position and she told me about her husband. My head was spinning with all of the in-home jobs I had tried to keep so I could stay home with the children. I needed more money than I could make at home, but Brian was only four. Could I wait until he was in kindergarten before going to work full time?

Opening Day of baseball and the annual parade! As we lined up outside the Village Hall, Donna convinced me to go inside and meet the mayor. I slowly shuffled up the stairs to his office, surveying my purple baseball shirt with large white letters, DYN-O-MITES, blue jeans and white gym shoes. This was quite an interview ensemble. He didn't seem surprised to see me. He remembered my husband from childhood. My eyes dropped to the floor at the mention of my husband's name. I hoped my face didn't show the pain that was now attached to any mention of him. We talked for a little while. He seemed like an honest man and asked for my resume. I went home after the Opening Day games and created a short version of a resume. He hired me. This must have been set up by God.

With God's guidance, I began this full time job in 1985. My husband continued to sleep on the couch – unable to hold a job – and unwilling to help with the children, so I hired my niece. I soon realized that I was supporting *five* children instead of four. I had tried every avenue thinkable – our priest, friends, counseling offices, his friends – but he wouldn't accept anyone's counsel.

PLANS FAIL WHEN THERE IS NO COUNSEL, BUT WITH ABUNDANT ADVISERS THEY ARE ESTABLISHED. — PROVERBS 15:22

I was concerned about working full time with Brian so young, but with my niece and then a neighbor's help, he adjusted well once he went to kindergarten. After I paid my niece or the neighbor, I barely had much left over, but it was more than I made staying at home. Working at the Village Hall helped me to get to know all the police officers personally. A few of them remembered me from the domestic disturbance calls. For the next several months, they told me when they stopped him for various reasons. I asked them not to give him any special treatment just because they knew me at work – he should deal with the consequences of his own actions. I began to feel sane at work (the opposite of what I felt at home). I could bring the children with me when they were sick and not able to go to school. The first summer was the toughest, change is always strange. But we got through it, even with each child coming down with the chicken pox.

My sister and I attended a mass for the sick that year. We wanted to pray for another sister who had been diagnosed with thyroid cancer. After the mass, we looked around for prayer partners to take our request of healing for our sister. They all broke into small groups.

"Let's not go over there," I pointed out to her. "Those people are dropping like flies when they are prayed over!"

We chuckled – healing prayer was new to both of us. We waited our turn and found a safe group – the people were either sitting or standing, no one was on the floor. We sat in a chair in the middle of them and asked for prayer for our sister. After the prayer, I began to weep. The dam inside me broke and tears flooded forward from extreme depths. I sobbed as one of the women asked what she could pray for me for that night.

"I don't know how long I can stay in my home," I muttered, in between my sobs. I looked up, searching for a ray of hope. "Do you think it would be okay with God if I leave?"

YET THIS I CALL TO MIND AND THEREFORE I HAVE HOPE; BECAUSE OF THE LORD'S GREAT LOVE WE ARE NOT CONSUMED, FOR HIS COMPASSIONS NEVER FAIL. THEY ARE NEW EVERY MORNING; GREAT IS YOUR FAITHFULNESS. I SAY TO MYSELF, THE LORD IS MY PORTION; THEREFORE I WILL WAIT FOR HIM. THE LORD IS GOOD TO THOSE WHOSE HOPE IS IN HIM, TO THE ONE WHO SEEKS HIM; IT IS GOOD TO WAIT QUIETLY FOR THE SALVATION OF THE LORD. — LAMENTATIONS 3:21-26

FIVE

A Nightmare Until I Changed It

I cowered in the corner of the soft blue sofa. It was two o'clock in the morning and I was tired, but unable to sleep. He would come home any minute. This time was different. I had locked him out. I didn't think I could bear one more night of having the house torn up. I hear it. A car door. He is approaching the front door of our small two bedroom rented house. He's beginning to swear as he pounds on the door.

"Lord, help me. Please make him go away."

He doesn't. He shakes the storm door until the glass breaks. He pounds and hollers louder and I call the police.

"There is a domestic disturbance outside my house."

I hear them talking on the porch. I open the door when I hear their voices. As one officer walks him to his car, the other one steps inside to talk to me. I see blood and broken glass on the porch.

"He has agreed to sleep in the car tonight. Legally, you can't lock him out. He lives here and has a legal right to come in. If you don't want him to come in, you have to do something about it legally."

This made me realize that my life would continue to be a

nightmare until I changed it. I was allowing this man to terrify me and my children.

Do something legally.

The officers leave. I lock the door and stumble to bed for several hours. I wake up early to clean up the broken glass and blood on the porch before the children awake. I wonder when the next episode will begin.

I continued to meet with the women from the retreat weekend and they encouraged me and prayed for me.

Do something legally.

I began talking to lawyers. They were expensive. I decided to talk to him about getting a separation instead of a divorce. He was downstairs, so I slowly approached him.

"Things have gotten out of hand here. No one is happy. I think it would be best for all of us if you and I separated for a little while."

I gulped as he stared at me.

"If you ever try to leave me, I'll kill the kids first and make you watch and then I'll kill you!" he shouted and glared at me with very strange eyes.

Those eyes didn't belong to the man I once knew. They looked dark as they stared at me to see if I believed what he was saying. I slowly walked upstairs and he followed me.

"I think I'll get a gun right now," he said as he walked out the door.

The weight of my body seemed to become an anchor as I struggled to gather the children. This weight was beyond a physical feeling. It seemed like the world had stopped and my head was spinning as I began to talk the children into getting into the car. I don't remember driving, but I arrived at a friend's home and told her what he said. She sat with me as I called the police and then his mother.

The police were on their way to find him and his mother's response was disappointing.

"Oh, my, you should never call the police. I put up with much worse than that and I never involved the police."

"I'm sorry for you," I responded.

I never spoke to her again about her son's behavior.

The police called me back at my friend's home. They had him and he didn't have a gun. They waited at our home until I returned with the children to process the incident. He was laughing as I entered the room.

"Do you believe her? What an idiot! She believed me!" he chuckled.

He laughed alone – the police officers stared at me with sadness.

When someone is under the influence of alcohol and/or drugs, anything can happen and any threats need to be taken seriously.

For six more months, I tiptoed around his drinking and fits. I gave an attorney a deposit through a loan from my credit union at work and made some small installments on a retainer. My life continued to be a challenge – trying to keep the children out of the house as much as possible – away from his abuse. When I wasn't at work, I was trying to bring some happiness into their lives. He was either drunk or hollering or withdrawn. He never sat with us as a family or even talked to us.

Even though I didn't think it could, his hollering and throwing things got worse. I woke up to see him snorting something – something that he bought using our grocery money! I called my mom again and begged her to let us come and live with her for a while. She hesitantly agreed. She didn't think I should try to raise four children by myself.

"It isn't really that bad, is it Mary?"

"Mom, it is. I wish I had a video camera."

November 4, 1986 should have been my 13th wedding anniversary. Instead, it is the anniversary of my exodus. He went out to watch Monday Night Football, so I thought we'd have two hours before his return. I had prepared the children earlier, told them that someday we would go to live with grandma because dad was sick and wasn't taking care of his sickness.

I never put him down in front of the children because they carried half of his genes. I wanted them to know that they were good people and their dad could be, but he wasn't making good choices. So, I told them that until dad made better choices, we needed to live apart from him. As it got closer to November and I was tucking them into bed, they would ask how soon we could go to live with grandma. They did not want to live with his choices any longer either.

Since I had spoken honestly with my children throughout our terror filled nights, they were excited about going to live with Grandma. I read in many books that children of alcoholics have an 80 percent chance of becoming alcoholics if they live with the person but a 50 percent chance if they are removed from living with the alcoholic. This was another motivating factor for me to get out of my marriage. I wanted to salvage my children from our horrendous existence and show them some peace – what Jesus promises us.

PEACE I LEAVE WITH YOU, MY PEACE I GIVE TO YOU. I DO NOT GIVE TO YOU AS THE WORLD GIVES. DO NOT LET YOUR HEARTS BE TROUBLED AND DO NOT BE AFRAID. — JOHN 14:27

I asked the children to pack garbage bags of whatever they would need. Only what they had to have. I called Donna because she had a station wagon. She was on her way over and I heard a car door. Erin looked out the window.

"Mom, it's dad."

My heart sank.

I pictured him doing what he promised. I went to the telephone and called the police. They knew me by name from many other calls. I asked them to wait outside and told them I would flash the porch light if he got violent. His rage was always worse when I involved the police.

I dropped to my knees and cried out to God for our lives.

"Father, I really didn't expect us to have to lose our lives to leave him. But, if this is what you choose, I know we will be happier in heaven. But, if possible, Father, could my children have a little more time to know life differently than this hell that they have lived in?"

HOW GRACIOUS HE WILL BE WHEN YOU CRY FOR HELP! AS SOON AS HE HEARS, HE WILL ANSWER YOU. — ISAIAH 30:19B

As I prayed, I bowed my head and waited. It was the scariest moment of my life. Someone was about to walk in my door who had promised to kill me and my children if we tried to leave. It was absolutely terrifying. But the thought of living with him one more minute had become so painful I had to try to escape.

So we waited. The dispatcher sent a car and, following my instructions, asked them to wait down the block until I flashed the porch light. The second hand on the clock moved like it was waddling through sludge. I watched the door, waiting for the knob to turn. My body was covered with sweat under my winter coat.

After what seemed like hours, though it was only five minutes, the front door didn't open and I heard another car door outside. Erin looked out again and saw Donna.

"Is she talking to your dad?"

"No, he isn't out there."

So, we didn't ask any questions.

We stuffed the bags into her car, the kids into my car, and waved to the police officers as we drove to my mom's for safekeeping. He called later that evening to say he walked to a friend's home after parking out in front. I told him that I couldn't live with his behavior and threats any longer. He said that scared him.

My mind juggled his word – SCARED – if he only knew the fear all of us had just living with him. He was not even aware of what he did or looked like when he was under the influence. Neither were any of our family members or friends.

My children are too precious to raise in the *hell* our life was and they are too precious for me to let his drinking turn them into future alcoholics. God guided me throughout that terrible marriage and the divorce. He gave me courage to face the threat of death for I believed he would kill us as we tried to leave and I remember our escape in November of 1986 as similar to Peter's escape from prison [ACTS 12:7-10]. We were guided by God's angels to safety.

I have learned much in my 12-step programs and can say with confidence that I did not know the man I married. He could not be honest or intimate with me because he buried hurts from his childhood and used alcohol to numb the pain. I buried hurts from my childhood and it has taken me years to understand who I am and why I do what I do. But, since working on myself, my life is going forward. I hope that someday he will work on himself and his life will move forward – just as I wish that all children of God escape the hold of past pain and learn to enjoy today – for life is such a beautiful gift.

With the strength of God, I was able to know that I was doing the right thing. And, no matter how many people told me that I couldn't do it on my own, I had to try to do it on my own – I had to raise my children as a single parent and, it was truly easier to raise four children without the abuse.

My mom had tried to get us back together. She didn't realize how bad it was, until an evening at her home about a month after we moved in when he arrived drunk, pounding and shouting. I called the police. She tried to reason with him before they came and finally gave up and sat with us until the police made him leave. She never asked me again to get back together with him.

After that, he only harassed us by telephone. I thanked God that I could now hang up on the verbal abuse! He would call every hour all night long – 10:00 PM, 11:00 PM, midnight, 1:00 AM, 2:00 AM, 3:00 AM, and hang up as soon as I answered. It took me several months before I gave myself permission to go to sleep with the phone unplugged. I had to learn boundaries from abuse – all kinds.

Mom adjusted her life to include the five of us. We began relating to each other a little differently. A wonderful man entered her life and they dated. She would bring me leftover stuffed mushrooms from their dinners. Dining out had become foreign to me. This man – Adolph – proposed to mom.

"If I marry him, at our ages, we will just be taking care of each other – and I don't need anyone else to take care of," Mom said.

"Well, mom, the kids and I need to move back near their school and my work. We won't be here much longer. You may want to consider marriage."

She loved to cook and he loved her cooking. It turned out to be a wonderful partnership.

It was difficult for the children to adjust at first. Even though we had been living in hell, it was all they knew and people usually accept unhappiness rather than change. One daughter wrote me a note asking me not to ever date anyone else or marry again because she couldn't handle it.

It didn't take long for them to appreciate being away from all the hollering and unhappiness.

One quiet evening, I was walking into the kitchen, searching for a snack as the children slept. Mom was out on a date. The phone rang. It was a call from a girlfriend from my youth. We had lived next door to each other from the time we were three until we turned 16. Our birthdays were one day apart and we had spent a lot of time together, even though we attended different schools. We had maybe spoken once or twice since high school. Her voice reminded me of another Mary. Had I really ever been a child?

After catching up on some of our life circumstances – like my current situation of moving back in with my mom, with four children, to try to get away from abuse – she asked if she could share something with me.

She began to read. I had been standing, but found a chair to gently slide into and, with my head down, absorbed her words. From somewhere deep inside me, tears began to flow. I knew her call and her words were a gift from God.

"Everyone longs to give themselves to someone – to have a deep soul relationship with another; to be loved thoroughly and exclusively. But God, to a Christian, says...

'No. Not until you are satisfied, fulfilled and content with being loved by Me alone; with giving yourself totally and unreservedly to Me alone; with having an intense, personal and unique relationship with Me. Discovering that, only in Me, is your satisfaction to be found will you be capable of the perfect human relationship that I have planned for you. You will never be united with another until you are united with Me; exclusive of anyone or anything else; exclusive of anyone to hear your desires or longings. I want you to stop planning, stop wishing and allow Me to give you the most thrilling plan existing – one you cannot imagine. I want you to have the best! Please allow me to give you the best. You just keep watching Me, experiencing the satisfaction that I am. Keep listening and learning the things I tell you. You just wait, that's all.

'Don't be anxious; don't worry. Don't look around at the things others have gotten or that I have given them. Don't look at the things you think you want. You just keep looking to Me, or you will miss what I want to show you. And then, when you are ready, I'll surprise you with a love far more wonderful than any you would dream of. You see, until you are ready and the one I have for you is ready (I am working even at this moment to have both of you ready at the same time); until you are both satisfied exclusively with Me and the life I've prepared for you, you won't be able to experience the love that exemplifies your relationship with Me. (For this is the perfect love.) And, dear child, I want you to have this most wonderful love. I want you to see, in the flesh, a picture of your relationship with Me. To enjoy, materially and concretely, the everlasting union of beauty, perfection and love that I offer you with Myself. Know that I love you utterly. I am God Almighty. Believe and be satisfied.'"

I lived with my mom for nine months. She was extremely generous to me. I was working full time and dropping the kids off at school on my way. They would walk to the library after school, where I would pick them up after work. After saving a little, I tried to find our own place.

The rejection I suffered searching for an apartment for us was new to me. Being rejected wasn't new, I had actually expected it from people. But how I was rejected was new to me. I never knew people had prejudices toward children. I was hung up on, laughed at, and called names when I mentioned I was a mom with four children looking to rent a two-bedroom apartment. I couldn't afford a three-bedroom apartment and struggled for months trying to find space for us.

Then, one day, through the help of Our Lord and prayer, I saw a newspaper ad for a condo. I didn't even know there were condos in my area and I needed to live there because I worked for the village and it had a residency requirement. This condo needed work, so it was priced low. It was two blocks from the kids' school and five blocks from my work – a perfect location. So, I went to look at it and with the money I saved living with my mom, plus a little financial help from her, I was able to get a mortgage with a payment of $400 per month. The apartment rent would have been $500. While there was $100 association fee, it was still the most reasonable way for the five of us to live.

I was told by my realtor that the residents held an association meeting to pass a rule on the number of occupants because they heard of my purchase and the size of my family. There were only two children in the whole building of 12 units and I represented four more children on the third floor. I can understand their apprehension. They couldn't pass the rule in time to stop my purchase so we moved into our first home with angry neighbors and with me not knowing if I could afford the $400-plus per month for this condo on a $17,000 a year salary.

I remember people at work asking if I needed help moving in. That was funny. You see, I just told them no thank you. The truth was there was nothing to move.

I had no furniture, not one fork or glass – nothing but the clothes we ran to my mom's with nine months earlier. I had a very generous sister who gave me a double bed for the girls' bedroom and a TV for the living room. Then, my ex-husband agreed to let me go back to the home we had rented and pick up the bunk beds for the boys and a rocker. So, they each had a bed to sleep in and I got a used sleeper sofa for myself in the living room. I purchased it at a garage sale and didn't notice that it only had three legs until I got it upstairs. A bowl became it's fourth leg.

The first night we slept in the condo I cried myself to sleep. After I locked the chain on the back door, this small home was heaven to me. I felt so safe and secure. There were locks downstairs and locks on the third floor. And, no one had permission to walk past those locks and verbally abuse, push around or hurt my children and me. No one could wake me up during the night ranting and throwing things anymore. A home where I could have peace when I locked the door at night.

I HAVE COME THAT THEY MAY HAVE LIFE, AND HAVE IT TO THE FULL. — JOHN 10:10B

I didn't care about the small size of the condo or the condition it was in; I only cared about what was inside – the four most precious people in the world to me – and God's peace. And I thanked Him, even as things got tougher financially, I thanked Him.

One thing that is important to me – which is His gift – is peace. When peace is taken out of your life because someone that has a legal right to live with you jeopardizes that peace; when you don't want to be in your home; when you don't want to be treated how you are being treated; when someone takes that away you have a right to get it back. God gives you a right to get it back.

I had finally attained God's peace. We were able to giggle and laugh without being ridiculed. We were able to be silly, we were able to love, to really feel love for each other. It was a wonderful beginning. I cried myself to sleep with tears of joy.

COMMAND THOSE WHO ARE RICH IN THIS PRESENT WORLD NOT TO BE ARROGANT NOR TO PUT THEIR HOPE IN WEALTH, WHICH IS SO UNCERTAIN, BUT TO PUT THEIR HOPE IN GOD WHO RICHLY PROVIDES US WITH EVERYTHING FOR OUR ENJOYMENT. — I TIMOTHY 6:17

SIX

A Good Life, But Not An Easy Life

Two months after I moved into the condo, my car died. I had nursed it for months, but it couldn't leak any more oil. It had reached its maximum quota for oil leaks! I knew the car wasn't in great condition when I left the marriage; I also knew there were two choices you had to make with cars. You either make payments on a new car or you pay a mechanic each month. That was my past experience with automobiles. So, instead of purchasing a used car without knowing how much it would cost me each month in repair bills, I decided to get an inexpensive new car and at least know what I was going to pay each month. Plus, the insurance was lower because the car was small. With the help of a friend, I got a Chevy Corsica, which seemed reasonable, and it had five seat belts – my only requirement. We were on our way at $240 a month. Added to my mortgage payment, that covered my entire paycheck.

Once my paycheck was gone on the mortgage and car payment, I needed to find out how to get extra money for food. It didn't take much convincing from others for me to apply for food stamps. I went down to the office and applied. My financial situation put me in their guidelines, so I moved to the next station and waited for them to call my name. As I waited, I saw individuals in wheelchairs, with crutches and with canes hobble up to register. As I watched them, I realized that I was in my thirties and I was physically able to work. Maybe my job wasn't paying enough, so I decided to get a second job instead of using food stamps. I walked out of the office without meeting with the caseworker and I applied at a couple of restaurants.

I heard that being a waitress was good money and I applied at Bailey's, but they only needed a hostess at five dollars an hour. I started there, but the Olive Garden called and I expected to make more like ten dollars an hour as a server, so I took the Olive Garden position. Being a waitress is a very humbling position. The way people treat you is unbelievable. It gave me a fantastic lesson on how to treat people who serve me. To this day, I never tip less than 20 percent because people don't realize that when you tip 15 percent, that's not what the server goes home with. (They have to give part of their tips to the bus boy and part to the bartender, which is called tipping out.) So, after tipping out, I usually went home with $35 for a five-hour shift if it was a good night. Some nights I would go home with $40 if it was a great night and other nights I would go home with $20 because it was slow. I worked Tuesdays and Thursdays from 5:00-10:00 PM. That worked out pretty well because it gave me every other night with the kids. I didn't want to leave too much responsibility on my oldest daughter, but she helped out tremendously during those lean years. She was very responsible for a 13-year-old. The absence of a parent will often create that scenario in a family.

The normal day during this season would go something like this:

up at 6:00 AM to exercise in front of the TV, shower and wake the children at 6:45 or so. We would go over homework, make lunches and be out the door together by 7:45 AM. I'd drop them off at school, drive to work and work from 8:00 AM-3:30 PM. I'd get home by 3:45, begin to fix something for dinner, put in a load of laundry (in the basement and I lived on the third floor – no elevator), feed the children and put the clothes in the dryer as I rushed to get to the Olive Garden by 5:00 PM. I'd work until 10:00 PM, then stop at Jewel on the way home to get groceries with the money I made that evening. Notes were left on the kitchen table of any trouble at school or with homework and I would climb into the couch and fall fast asleep. It was a very busy time and we were grateful that school was so close. It was a good life but not an easy life. There were many nights that I would fall asleep crying from exhaustion, but I would never hesitate to smile knowing this was a much better life than I had left. I didn't have money, but I had smiles on my children's faces and peace in our home. Oh, they wrestled and fought like brothers and sisters do. I tried to discipline correctly but made some mistakes. I saved some notes from my favorite discipline: they had to write an apology and a compliment to a person they had called a name. Something like "I'm sorry I called you a dork – you are good at baseball."

They also had to deal with the rejection of their father. He wouldn't send child support because he wanted it to be difficult for me because he said that I had wanted this.

I hung around with four other women going through a divorce the same year. We called ourselves the *Big D Club*; not something to be proud of but it was something we had in common.

We went out to talk maybe once a month – sometimes to talk or dance – to take a break from parenting. I was the only one of the five of us not getting child support and the only one with four children. The other women had either one or two children each. So, there were times when I was on the pity pot. The pity pot of "Why, God? This just doesn't seem fair!"

But, He would show me, time and time again, that He would provide for me. I think He was teaching me to trust in Him as my provider. One Tuesday I had had a *long* day at work. I rushed home, put something on the table for the children to eat, gave instructions, ran downstairs and began a load of laundry, ran out the door just in time to get to the parking lot of the Olive Garden at five o'clock. I sat in the parking lot, took a deep breath and realized I couldn't move. I began to cry out to the Lord.

"Lord, I can't move. I can't walk. I am so exhausted. I can't serve these people. But, if I don't, we don't have food the next couple of days." I took another deep breath and said, "You have to be me tonight, Lord. You have to be my hands, my feet and my mouth – you have to serve these people. I have nothing more to give."

I dried my tears and walked in. The next thing I can remember was standing in Jewel purchasing groceries. I do not remember serving people that night at all. He did what I had to do physically, because I had nothing left.

IN HIS LOVE AND MERCY HE REDEEMED THEM; HE LIFTED THEM AND CARRIED THEM. — ISAIAH 63:9B

I'm grateful for the many times He carried me. I was in Toys 'R Us on my way to the Olive Garden one night before Christmas. I was trying to purchase a Game Boy. It was the only thing Kevin wanted and it was all he was getting that year. They wouldn't put it on my VISA.

My card had a limit of $500 and I purposefully had that limit to keep myself in line. I had one charge card and that was for our winter coats, shoes, anything out of the ordinary monthly expenses, Easter dresses, Christmas presents and the like. Well, my VISA was already at $420 and they wouldn't let me charge the Game Boy. How humiliating standing at the checkout counter of Toys 'R Us and being turned down from purchasing Kevin's Christmas present! It was the last Christmas gift I had to get that year.

The children didn't always get what they wanted for the holidays or birthdays. When Brian wanted a GI Joe play set, I couldn't afford it and purchased an imitation one for half the price at Woolworth. I didn't think he would know the difference. Well, he knew the difference. He knew exactly what he wanted and what I substituted it with wasn't what he wanted and he never did play with it. To this day, I have searched the Web for that play set and hope to find it someday for him to play with alongside his children! I really felt terrible because I disappointed him when I wasn't able to get him the one thing he wanted.

KEEP YOUR LIVES FREE FROM THE LOVE OF MONEY AND BE
CONTENT WITH WHAT YOU HAVE. — HEBREWS 13:5A

Sometimes, if you don't get what you want, you will get what you need from the Lord. Brian used to ask for a basketball net outside. Living in a condo, I couldn't possibly provide one. I would have to tell them time and time again that I couldn't afford a house. Where we were living was all I could do and it didn't include a basketball net. Since children don't really understand finances, I sometimes had to repeat again and again that we couldn't have things others had. Sometimes I would get on the pity pot and get mad at God – cry out to Him – can't you help? Can't you just find a small two-bedroom house with a little driveway so I can get a basketball net? It was never what He wanted for my children. He chose for us to accept living in the condo with a shared driveway.

One of the things I was learning was acceptance. There is real joy in acceptance instead of desiring things God has not allowed. I finally sat down with Brian.

"This looks like our life, Bri. This is the home I can provide on my income. I need you to accept that, someday, when you are older, you can get a home with a basketball net. I have to accept that this is the best I can do and I want to stop feeling bad that I can't provide a basketball net for you. This life is okay. This home is good. But, it does not include a basketball net."

He accepted that talk and seemed to understand. He never again asked for one during those years.

BE JOYFUL IN HOPE, PATIENT IN AFFLICTION, FAITHFUL IN PRAYER. — ROMANS 12:12

SEVEN

The Lord Provided

I couldn't afford plumbers, electricians or painters, so I learned a lot. I repaired the bathroom wall where tiles were falling off with green board, I flooded the kitchen trying to repair a leaky faucet (and the kitchen below me), I installed a new kitchen floor myself using those self-adhesive vinyl squares. None of my jobs were perfect, but I read some books, talked to people and tried things. I shouldn't have done one electrical job myself. I found out later that with the grace of God I narrowly escaped electrocuting myself.

I tried things, the Lord provided and we got by. The Lord provided in ways that were beyond just handing me an easier life. He taught me.

I was asked to be on a committee at church for the divorced and widowed. We met as a group to orchestrate social events. We were asked to work on a way to encourage individuals to get together. As the committee met, we would sometimes share a little about ourselves. It was a good group, about eight of us. We met a couple of times and as we got to know each other, we would share some of our pain.

One man talked a long time about the painful loss of his wife. One particular evening, I shared that my daughter Erin was not able to join her class on the eighth grade trip. The class was going to Washington, DC. It was very difficult for me to accept, but I decided Our Lord didn't want her to go on the trip because I had exhausted any possible way of coming up with the $300 she needed. I couldn't borrow any more from my mom and my VISA wouldn't take it. And as I cried I shared my thoughts with them.

"The hard part is, you know Our Lord has a reason for everything. Accepting that she can't go isn't as hard for me as it will be explaining it to her. I'm sure there are other kids not going – there has to be. But all of her close friends are going."

After I shared that with the group, I felt a big relief. I had let it out. I had given it to the group and to God. I went home that night and talked to her. She did understand. I knew she would. She was always very intelligent and responsible. She knew I was doing the best I could but I couldn't come up with the $300.

When I went to work the next day, a gentleman from the group walked into my office. He had never visited me before and I was surprised, but even more surprised when he handed me an envelope.

"You know," he said with frustration, "I couldn't fall asleep last night until I promised God that I would bring you $300 to send your daughter to Washington."

"Really?"

"You must have some connection," he said.

"Well, we all do! But I thought God was saying she couldn't go, and he's using you to send her!"

"All I know is that I tossed and turned, tossed and turned until I agreed to go to the bank as soon as they opened."

Months later, he and I were able to laugh about it. It was a lot of money. It was God's work and God had nudged him and he had listened. And I was so grateful and so was my daughter.

There were many times I hit the bottom and I didn't know how to get up. But, thanks to Him, I didn't stay there too long because I believed He had a purpose and a reason for everything and He was teaching me something.

I remember reading M. Scott Peck's book, *The Road Less Traveled*, and the new perspective it gave me on dealing with life's challenges.

"Life is difficult.

This is a great truth, one of the greatest truths. It is a great truth because once we truly see this truth, we transcend it. Once we truly know that life is difficult—once we truly understand and accept it—then life is no longer difficult. Because once it is accepted, the fact that life is difficult no longer matters.

Most do not fully see this truth that life is difficult. Instead they moan more or less incessantly, noisily or subtly, about the enormity of their problems, their burdens, and their difficulties as if life were generally easy, as if life should be easy. They voice their belief, noisily or subtly, that their difficulties represent a unique* kind of affliction that should not be and that has somehow been especially visited upon them, or else upon their families, their tribe, their class, their nation, their race or even their species, and not upon others. I know about this moaning because I have done my share.

Life is a series of problems. Do we want to moan about them or solve them? Do we want to teach our children to solve them?"

Another challenge came when I was driving Erin to a job she held at age 15 at a restaurant. Some teenagers drove alongside us and as they moved in front of our car in their lane, they threw beer bottles in our lane. We were both going around 35 mph and there was nowhere for me to swerve to avoid the broken glass. I took my daughter to work and picked her up a couple of hours later and hadn't noticed any fragments on my tires. I was excited. It looked like we had avoided any tire damage. At work the next day, checking my tires again, I was thrilled that they were inflated and I thanked the Lord for that close call. About an hour later, a police officer came to my desk.

"How did you get to work?" she asked.

"My car."

"Have you seen it lately?"

"Well, I've only been at work an hour."

"Come here and look."

We walked to the parking lot and there it sat – all four tires were as flat as pancakes. I looked at her in disbelief and told her about the night before and she mentioned slow leaks. I went to my office and wept. It was about ten days before Christmas and I had capped my VISA already that year. I never really told people how I lived week-to-week with my paycheck and how little money the five of us had. Well, I started to tell her how little money I had, and apologized for crying.

"I'll call my mom – she's been there before and I have always paid her back," I said.

"I have a friend who works at a gas station nearby and he'll give you a good price."

And he did. He quoted me a good price and towed the car in. Then I called my mom and thank the Lord, she again offered to help. She was willing to lend me the money and I breathed a sigh of relief. I called later that day to see when my car would be ready and they said it had already been picked up and I thought, "Oh, terrific." This woman police officer really went way out of her way to help me. I went to find her.

"Thanks so much for picking up my car. Where's the receipt?"

"Come here, I'll show you," she said.

We walked to the fire escape on the second floor overlooking the parking lot. I looked down at my car as people started gathering around me. There were four large red bows, one on each tire, and people gathered around saying "It's a wonderful life, Mary." They had taken up a collection. Now I was crying tears of joy. It was so humbling and I was so in awe of God and how He works through people. Two days later, a gentleman came up to me at the copy machine.

"Oh, Mary, I wanted to donate. Who's collecting for your tires?"

"I don't know who you pay, but thank you."

It was an awesome gift and I'll never forget it. There were so many wonderful, wonderful times that Our Lord provided but it seemed that when I was in the depths, not knowing which way to turn, He would come up with a solution.

After working at the Olive Garden, a friend of mine suggested serving banquets for a second job and she got me into the Hyatt Regency. What a wonderful second job. I could bring home $100 on one Saturday night, so I only needed to be away from the kids once a week and still earn enough for our groceries. I was thrilled. The only problem was that we lifted heavy trays of expensive dishes and coffee pots. So, after a Saturday night, I often could not get out of bed on Sunday morning – my legs wouldn't move. But, by Sunday afternoon, everything was fine and I worked that job until my daughters were able to get baby-sitting jobs.

Once they provided a little income, I was able to stop a second job and concentrated on making more money at my full-time job. I went to seminars, honed my skills and asked for raises. Eventually, I was able to only work the one full-time job and keep us afloat. I had also worked part-time at a Fitness Club and it was wonderful because I could bring the kids with me and they would play racquetball while I worked the desk. I got to work out for free and exercise was a tremendous release for me.

One morning I was driving the girls to school in an automobile that was struggling. I had learned a little about an alternator – what I needed and couldn't afford yet. It began to chug as I turned left at the last stoplight before school.

"Even though it's cold outside, I need to turn off the heat, the wipers, the radio and anything else that uses the battery. That way, we may make it to school."

We chugged another block and turning left again, over the median, was too much for it. Dead – right in the middle of four lanes of traffic – straddling the median strip.

"Well, girls, it looks like we have to push the…" as I laid my hand across the seat and turned to look at them.

My eyes met an empty back seat and heard the closing of two doors simultaneously. They had darted. I slowly stepped out on the pavement with my skirt and pumps, moved around to push and there was a young man – an angel, I am sure – ready to push. So we pushed at the side of the car and maneuvered it into the school parking lot. He was gone before I could thank him and the girls approached me once I got into the school to use the phone. How much embarrassment could someone allow – pushing your mother's car into school – what humiliation would that have tortured them with?

I had made an agreement with God that I would keep them in a Catholic school as long as possible. I wanted them in a school that spoke of Jesus. Until the school told me they couldn't return because of my inability to keep up with tuition, they would attend. At one time, even though I had two paying jobs, I also worked part-time at the rectory. I did office work for the school and church in order to get some money credited to my tuition balance while they were in Catholic grammar school.

As they approached high school, I wanted the girls to go to an all girls Catholic high school and the boys to go to an all boys Catholic high school. I knew there was no way I could come up with the tuition. In fact, I remember signing the first tuition contract for Erin's school because my entire body shook. I was trembling when I looked at the amount I was promising to pay that year. I knew I couldn't make those payments.

PUT YOUR HOPE IN GOD, WHO RICHLY PROVIDES US WITH EVERYTHING FOR OUR ENJOYMENT. — 1 TIMOTHY 6:17B

I do have one friend who was like a grandpa to my children and attended a lot of their baseball games. He would sometimes send small donations to each school in my children's names. Sometimes the children worked programs with the school, like cleaning classrooms, in order to get tuition assistance. Once they were sophomores, my daughters were able to hold jobs and each of them paid $100 a month toward their tuition balance.

When Kevin took the entrance exam for high school, he scored as one of the highest in the group and earned a $1,000 scholarship for each of his four years as long as he maintained his grades. When it was announced that he had received the award, he told me to "cool it" until we reached a deserted hallway outside the gym. Then I exploded like a high school cheerleader. And, he did maintain his grades for all four years!

We all did everything possible, but the total tuition costs for four children for twelve years of schooling each could only be explained as a miracle. I am so grateful because I believed that if they heard of Jesus every day in school, they would have a better chance of becoming adults who knew how important He was to life.

I also tried to teach them honesty. One summer I remember going with friends to a nearby community pool. They had passes and offered for some of us to use their passes, as they knew my financial situation. But, I told my children that wouldn't be honest. I had $20 left until my paycheck on Friday and it took every bit of it to enter the pool. Swimming was something we never had a chance to do.

On the way home, the kids mentioned that now we didn't have enough money to get burgers. I had told them we may be able to get McDonald's burgers another time, but I was sure I could find something in the cabinet for dinner. I almost always had spaghetti noodles and a can of tomato sauce in the cabinet as I purchased a lot of it when it was on sale. We drove home and I dropped them off first while I ran into work to check on some telephone messages. When I returned to our building Brian came running up to me with two $100 bills in his hand. He was so excited. My ex-husband had stopped by and given Brian two $100 bills. He rarely paid child support and when he did, it came through the court system – never cash – so I knew this was a gift from God.

I looked at the children and said, "see how the Lord has provided ten fold of the $20 we spent honestly today!"

We excitedly went to McDonald's and celebrated.

When school began each fall, we needed new shoes, backpacks, and numerous school supplies. The list seemed endless for a parent with no extra weekly funds. One September, I opened an envelope from my sister in California. It was marked PHOTOS and I thought how precious. We rarely saw each other and I anxiously opened the envelope and as I did, five $100 bills fell into my hand. I almost fell down in the hallway! She told me her husband had received a bonus and she wanted to share it with me. She marked the envelope "photos" to fool any possible mail thieves! It is difficult to describe the tremendous feeling of gratitude I had toward her and towards God for knowing my needs and supplying a way of meeting them. I knew that the Lord had prompted my sister and her husband to send that money because the Lord was the one who knew what was going on in my life.

There were times when my mom would send me $50 in the mail.

"I don't know what prompted me to send it," she would say.

"Mom, it was the Holy Spirit."

As an example, she would mail $50 on a Monday and on Thursday of that week, as I opened the mail, I would need $50 for a car repair bill or something that came up. I also was blessed with a brother and sister-in-law who found out how tough my finances were and started sending me anything extra they had once their monthly bills were paid. The Lord was putting me on people's minds two and three days before things happened to me – He was providing for us. He is providing for us every step of the way and once we realize this, life is so much easier.

THEY HAD A FEW SMALL FISH, HE GAVE THANKS FOR THEM AND TOLD THE DISCIPLES TO DISTRIBUTE THEM. THE PEOPLE ATE AND WERE SATISFIED. — MARK 8:6-7

I was still a novice at this. I was so in awe of Him. But I was not fully convinced He was totally providing everything because life was still difficult. I was working a lot, my children were working a lot and we waited for things to get easier. Time and time again, I felt like one of His apostles, who saw Him do miracles, yet doubted His authority, power and provision.

How many times does He have to provide for us before we truly realize He has been with us all along and He knows our every step? He takes care of us before something needs to be taken care of – He provides prior to our need.

Besides the difficulties the children were experiencing financially, they were also experiencing many difficult times having to visit their father. He was still drinking and the courts agreed to my request for Sunday visitation. I believed that would be the safest day for them to be with him. There were some Sundays when they refused to get out of the car to go visit him and I had to force them to go. It was so difficult for all of us emotionally. I was afraid if they didn't go in for the Sunday visit, he could make trouble in court to see them other times. I took them to a counselor once, to help them deal with all this pain, but couldn't afford the visits and had to stop. I had hoped, over the years as they grew, that they would go to counseling to have healing from the issues that can surface from the lack of a relationship with a birth father.

BLESSED IS HE WHOSE HELP IS THE GOD OF JACOB, WHOSE HOPE IS IN THE LORD HIS GOD, THE MAKER OF HEAVEN AND EARTH, THE SEA AND EVERYTHING IN THEM – THE LORD REMAINS FAITHFUL FOREVER…THE LORD LIFTS UP THOSE WHO ARE BOWED DOWN. — PSALM 146:5-6

EIGHT

Get Rid Of The Baggage

God provided a wonderful gift to my mental health. Over the years of this marriage, I was torn down, verbally abused, so much so that I believed the put downs and my self-image was battered. As I began to date after my marriage, I was still attracted to men who gave me little attention and were usually very selfish. I felt so unworthy of anyone's attention, that I would accept dates with people who weren't emotionally healthy.

I know that now, but at that time, dating men with problems was all I was used to. Actually, they were who I was comfortable with. The man I dated the longest didn't drink, so I thought I had finally made a good choice. However, it turned out he was addicted to marijuana – but it took me two and one-half years and being engaged to him before I found out he wasn't good for me. Ellen didn't like him at all, but she didn't like anyone I dated. So, I didn't take her dislike too seriously and it turns out she has a great gift of discernment.

Single parenting is so difficult and it was so nice to have someone to talk to about the concerns and burdens as well as the joys of my day.

It was so nice to have someone I thought gave me good advice and counsel for handling the children. When you make all the decisions yourself, you begin to get a little hard at being open to suggestions – even from the kids – and it was good to have someone else to process things with. I really did respect this man and appreciated the love he had for his family, for me and for my children.

It all changed while playing cards. His son used a mirror to see Ellen's hand and when caught, their family laughed at how wise that seemed. I disagreed. I believed in honesty at all times and didn't find it humorous but found it something to reprimand. This created quite a discussion but Our Lord used it to bring me to a beautiful chapter of my life.

I went to a counselor at an office recommended and paid for by my employer. I still remember sitting in the waiting room thinking, "What am I doing here?" I was very nervous. I thank God that I kept that appointment for I met a counselor named Jay. We talked for about an hour about my past relationships and this present one. During this meeting, he asked what I believed I was teaching my children.

"To be good to others."

"I think you are going to raise four martyrs," he said, "When people begin to stop taking care of their responsibilities, others usually enable them by picking up the pieces for them. Just what did you expect your husband to accomplish each day by the end of your marriage?"

"All he had to do was breathe," was my response.

This confirmed his diagnosis of my problems and he introduced me to the term CODEPENDENT. I had never heard of it. He said he would be glad to see me two more times because work would pay for three visits, but he didn't think I needed a counselor as much as I needed education on codependency. He gave me his card with an 800 number to locate a support group in my area for Codependents Anonymous (CoDA), a fellowship of men and women whose common purpose is to develop healthy relationships. He also recommended a book called *Codependent No More* by Melody Beattie.

I left there pretty charged that there was something that could help me. I went to the library and looked up this author and found three books she authored which I quickly consumed. They changed my life. As I read her books, it was as though someone was looking directly into my life. My marriage was described in there, my relationship with other men, my relationships with my parents, my children, my boss – it was just so eye-opening that there was someone out there that understood and knew why I did what I did. But, the biggest shocker was, there was help!

I didn't even know I needed help and I found help! I found out I didn't relate in a healthy way! I felt I needed to talk to other people about it and there weren't people I knew who had much 12-step knowledge. I looked up the CoDA meetings, found one in Elmhurst not too far from my home and went every Monday night at 7 o'clock. I remember it was from 7:00-8:00 PM because I made a commitment to attend in order to take care of myself. I went to these meetings for approximately two years and I learned so much. I learned so much about behavior, I learned so much about 12-stepping, I learned so much about relationships, *and* I learned so much about Mary.

INSTRUCT A WISE MAN AND HE WILL BE WISER STILL; TEACH A RIGHTEOUS MAN AND HE WILL ADD TO HIS LEARNING. — PROVERBS 9:9

I broke off the engagement with the gentleman whose son cheated at cards, and finally, the whole friendship with him. I journeyed into healing of my past. I read a book called "Healing the Inner Child" and I did remember many painful childhood events. The reason I did that is because I've learned that in remembering, bringing those forward, you can forgive those who have hurt you, you can go forward then to be a new, whole person. You get rid of the baggage. We all carry baggage, whether or not we like it, but we can decide how much we want to carry into new relationships. I was carrying a lot of baggage into new relationships. Through CoDA, I learned how to get rid of the baggage so when I entered a new relationship, I could respond in a healthy way to situations and not a response based on what someone else had done to me years ago.

It's an amazing journey if you want to take it. If you find yourself enabling or taking care of people who can take care of themselves or if you are controlling or manipulating others, try CoDA. You can become free of manipulating others. We don't need to have the answers for everyone else. And, we don't need to have anyone else in our life to have a full life. Codependents take care of other people, feel sorry for others, are hard workers, dedicated to others, and very nurturing individuals. Codependents are wonderful to have around unless they do things for others that the others should be doing for themselves.

After my divorce, if I walked into a room and there were 100 men and 99 of them were healthy, I would be attracted to the one who was unhealthy. I was a magnet for taking care of people.

By the grace of God, I learned the things I needed to learn through CoDA and I grew in how to relate to people and how to identify what is a healthy and what is a codependent relationship. After breaking up with this gentleman who I had dated for several years, thanks to the knowledge CoDA gave me and my ability to recognize that this was not a healthy relationship, I was asked out by another gentleman.

His name was David and his company did business with the village. At first, I said, no thank you. I didn't trust my ability to choose who to date yet. I wanted a little time. A month later, I saw him again.

"Whatever happened to our cup of coffee?" I asked.

We went out to dinner and had a very nice evening. I didn't know much about him, but on our second visit, we found out we were both 12-steppers. Both of our first marriages had ended because of alcoholism.

He had gone to Al-Anon and I had gone to CoDA. I distinctly remember our second evening together because of one of his questions during dinner.

"What would you like out of this friendship?" David asked.

Meaning, him and me – a guy I hardly knew. I looked at him and laughed at first.

"Before I went through 12-stepping, before I learned about Mary and the things that she needs to make life work – and they don't involve other people – I probably would have said something like: 'Oh, I would like to someday get to know you better and maybe you can help me raise my kids. Maybe we can get married someday.' And I would have gone on and on about wants, needs, dreams and projections from a relationship when I don't even have any idea really what type of person you are. But, now, I'll tell you what I would like out of this friendship. Because I've changed with what I want out of life and everything is different. So, if you and I have a good time tonight and you call again and want to go out next Saturday night – that would be great. But, if you never call again, if I never hear from you and my name doesn't exist in your vocabulary, I'm still going to have a great Saturday night."

He just looked at me. He really wasn't sure what to say.

"You see, what's changed in me is that I don't need you or anyone else to make my life happy. God and I make my life happy. And, I'm going to enjoy my life, with or without you being a part of it. So, I really don't have any expectations from you or from this friendship."

This was eye opening for me and for him. He had already started having friendships with other women and he wasn't quite sure what he wanted, but he knew what he didn't want. I think it helped both of us. In fact, a few visits later, he asked if I wanted his car phone number.

"No, there isn't any reason that I would have to get a hold of you in your car. Plus, I know it's more expensive to call you in your car. I can always reach you at home or at work if I need to."

He was surprised. He was used to women who wanted a little bit more, and more, and I didn't. I think that is what kept him calling me.

I was different. I wasn't needy. I was a single woman with four children and I didn't need anything from any man. I had learned that my life was good and that I could make it good for my children without a relationship with a male in it. I didn't need a male role model for my children. They were going to have them in school, in sports, or whatever they would be involved in. They had a father. They didn't need another father. He wasn't the best one, but he was their father and they were going to have to deal with that. So, I stopped the thinking I had for many years. I started with healthy thinking and I thank the Lord for CoDA and the things this program taught me about Mary and her behavior.

I taught my children many things I learned from CoDA. I remember one day when I walked in the kitchen door after a really difficult day at work. I was exhausted mentally and I surveyed the dishes in the kitchen sink and the kids running around after each other.

"Doesn't anyone notice that there are dishes in the sink that need to be cleaned up? Can't anyone help out without me having to make a big deal out of it?" I asked in a *motherly* tone.

Before I could continue my second suggestion – or command – Ellen spoke up without missing a beat.

"Wait a minute, mom. I don't think you are mad at us. I think something happened at work today."

Now, she learned that through our discussions from my 12-stepping on misdirected anger. I was totally frustrated from work. I came home and tried to take out my frustration on them and their behavior. It wasn't the dishes in the sink. I mean, I wasn't happy about them, but they were not the cause of my frustration. I knew it would really help her to understand misdirected anger because if someone is shouting at you, it might not be from anything that you did; a *very* valuable lesson.

My self-esteem had been torn down by the words of others over the years. I left my marriage without any self-esteem and built it back up through CoDA. After CoDA, I expected more from people in relationships with me. I learned to not have relationships with people who did not treat me with respect. That was a difficult concept for me. The easiest way to say this is, if you are in someone's line of fire – if someone is badgering you, hollering at you, making fun of or jokes about you, or verbally putting you down – *you have a choice!*

You can stay there and take it or you can remove yourself. When my ex-husband badgered me, whether it was physically or verbally, I didn't know I could leave. I never removed myself from the premises. I never hung up on him during the divorce when he called and hollered. He used the phone often to harass me – especially with hang-ups all during the night.

There was a gentleman at work who spoke very loudly and shouted at people. We were on the phone once and he was shouting at me and I hung up.

"We must have been disconnected," he said when he called back.

"No, we weren't. Until you talk in a normal tone, you can't have a conversation with me because my ear hurts from your last words. That's how loud you were. And I choose to speak with people who control the tone of their voice."

I claimed the right of whom I would and would not allow into my personal space. I learned to respect Mary and I wanted to have relationships with others who also respected her.

I tried to teach my children that once you have raised your voice, you have lost control. So you need to calm yourself down and come back when you can speak in a normal tone. Shouting is very, very common and it's accepted by most but I don't believe it is God's way of communicating. I believe we are supposed to speak kindly to each other and speak softly.

PLEASANT WORDS ARE A HONEYCOMB, SWEET TO THE SOUL AND HEALING TO THE BONES. — PROVERBS 16:24

It's not that I shouted before CoDA, but I can say that I raised my voice. But I learned from CoDA that once you do that, you have lost control and you need to remain in control if you are going to be in a relationship. People can choose to be in relationship with you.

I never knew I had a choice.

I felt that anybody who had a relationship with me had a

relationship with me and however others wanted to treat me they were able to treat me. I was pretty much a doormat. Through CoDA, I learned to respect myself enough to choose who to be in a relationship with. And, I am very honest with people and I will tell them whether what they are doing is something I will accept or not.

Some people were very taken aback, especially individuals who were used to the *old* Mary.

I remember when a former boyfriend and I were at a pool, during my years of learning about behavior through CoDA, and I was first learning to listen to my feelings. He watched a girl for a long time and I commented how I thought his stare was longer than necessary.

"It wouldn't bother 99 percent of other women," he said.

"Well, it bothers me, so you should go date the other 99 percent."

It was the first time I stood up for something that bothered me and didn't fall for the other person telling me it shouldn't.

AND HOPE DOES NOT DISAPPOINT US, BECAUSE GOD HAS POURED OUT HIS LOVE INTO OUR HEARTS BY THE HOLY SPIRIT, WHOM HE HAS GIVEN US. — ROMANS 5:5

NINE

A Love Of God's Word

I continue to thank the Lord for CoDA and the 12-step programs. One aspect of these programs uses the term HIGHER POWER. When I would talk about Jesus Christ in that atmosphere, many people didn't know Him and it inhibited me because I realized they were on a different plane than I was – their higher power wasn't real. Their higher power was vague, but my higher power had a name. He was my Lord and Savior, Jesus Christ.

In the meantime, David continued to call. He went to a different church and his church had a 12-step program that included the Lord and Scripture. It was an amazing way to work through the 12 steps. He and I had stopped seeing each other for a while because his ex-wife had left him and the children, but his divorce was not final when we met. We decided to stop socializing until his divorce was final. The divorce proceedings were being prolonged because she suffered from alcoholism and was not able to always make attorney appointments or court dates. Plus, as a Christian, he was trying to save his marriage and we would pray together for her to come back to her family.

I was born and raised as a Catholic and I felt I had a relationship with God, except during the time when I had lost so many loved ones and walked away for about a year. Other than that, I thought I walked pretty close to God and alongside Him. After the weekend when I was "reborn" and accepted Him as my Savior and Lord, I became a Eucharistic Minister and a reader at church. I devoted much more time to God and loved learning Scripture. God truly became my best friend.

When I met David and his church, Christian Reformed, he said we were worlds apart. I knew that Catholics and Protestants in Ireland fought, but I really didn't know the difference between churches. As we began dating, we saw each other's love for the Lord and our day-to-day relationship with the Lord was very similar but our churches were different. But the differences in our churches were not as extreme as each person had thought them to be.

I often said to him, "We should look at what the churches do alike, instead of looking at all the differences."

FOR THERE IS ONE GOD AND ONE MEDIATOR BETWEEN GOD AND MEN, THE MAN CHRIST JESUS. — 1 TIMOTHY 2:5

What became clear to me is that there is a lot of good in all churches that acknowledge Jesus Christ as Savior and Lord and utilize His Word, the Bible. There may be legalism, idol worship and false teachings in some churches, among other sins. Churches are made up of *people* and we are all sinners. The issue is finding a church where you are nourished and fed through The Word of God, the Bible. Scripture is so powerful. I don't know if I would have developed a tremendous love of His Word through the Catholic church I attended but I did hear it taught and preached. I studied it, though, in the Christian Reformed church.

I would go home from the service and look up verses that were quoted and question things the pastor said. There is still so much for me to learn because His Word is so alive and active that the more I study it, the more I know *I don't know* and the more I want to apply it to my life. I will always love the Catholic church and miss some of its traditions like kneeling and communion every day. But, I will be eternally grateful for the depth of my walk with the Lord that the Christian Reformed church taught me by teaching me to love and study Scripture.

I thanked the Lord, and I mentioned this to David for introducing me to a love of God's Word through the teachings and study of the Bible. Whatever the Lord had planned for our friendship, I received a great gift and that was the importance of seeking out churches to continue to grow. To seek out the Word of God and where it is preached and what road will bring you, personally, closer to Him. What He is going to use in *your* life to draw *you* closer to His Truth.

As we started dating, once his divorce was final, I noticed that there was something I had not dealt with – the break up of my marriage. He had been asked for accountability in his relationship with me from his church, so they requested information on the break up of my marriage, in order to see if they were Biblically able to condone us dating. I was a little offended writing this out, as I felt that they did not trust that I was smart enough to know whether or not to end my marriage. I believed I had a good reason for ending my marriage. But, you see, in answering their questions, it was growth for me. Every process you go through, just like the annulment process I went through for the Catholic church helps.

The annulment process in the Catholic church is an interesting one. I worked through this process before learning in depth about 12-step programs and feel it can be considered a 12-step program for a failed marriage.

First, after your divorce is final, you approach a deacon or priest in your parish who helps you initiate the process. You are asked a few questions and given some advice. If the reason for your divorce is understood, the deacon or priest initiates paperwork and the process begins. You receive your application with many questions. You can answer them in one word or in many sentences and take as long as you like to turn them in. You also turn in the names of three witnesses; individuals who knew you throughout your entire marriage, and they are sent questions. They also contact your ex-spouse with questions.

After all the paperwork is completed and turned in, you meet with a field advocate, an advisor who discusses your marriage, your divorce and your future. This individual spends some time with you and discusses your answers on your application. In my case, you then meet with a psychologist.

My annulment was granted on the grounds that my ex-husband never lived up to his vows. He never took any responsibility as a marriage partner and so the vows were considered null and void.

It was a fantastic process and I just about wrote a book answering their questions. One of the interesting things that came out of the process for me was a psychiatric evaluation.

I went downtown to an office of the Archdiocese of Chicago and read inkblots and answered questions and as I was answering questions, I started to notice that number 136 was identical to 12 and I looked back and sure enough, the question about the red handkerchief was repeated. So, I thought they were looking for consistency and went back and found my answer for number 12 to answer 136. It was fun for me.

As the psychiatrist looked over my answers and we sat together at the end, I talked to him about my friends who got an annulment who did not have a psychiatric evaluation.

"Yes," he said.

"Oh, I thought I was called here as part of the regular process."

"No."

"Then, why did I have to take one?"

"We read your papers and called you in because with all you've gone through in your marriage, we think you are a masochist."

"What?"

"Do you know what a masochist is?"

"As far as I know, it is a person who likes pain."

"Yes. We don't think you would have stayed in your marriage as long as you did if you didn't enjoy pain."

Well, you could have knocked me over with a feather. I answered him softly.

"You are representing the church. I stayed married because I promised God that I would marry for better or for worse. I was living in the worse and waiting for it to get better. I stayed married because of God and now, you, representing the church and my God, are telling me I stayed too long??"

"Nobody would have put up with this."

"Well, welcome to my world. I did. And I'm not nuts and I don't like pain."

When I went home, I felt like I lost 30 pounds. The church not only granted my annulment, they told me I had put up with too much!

I wanted to share this because the annulment process also gave me the freedom to remarry. Now, I never wanted to and really didn't think I would, but yet, I wanted to be open to whatever God's plan was.

When David and I started seeing each other on a regular basis and we went to church together, we found out we had much in common and quite a bit different in our backgrounds. I was a "divorced Catholic with four children" which meant I was also not Dutch. Most of the people were wonderful to me and most of my friends were wonderful to him, but it is interesting how the evil one tricks us to notice how rejected we are by a few instead of how accepted we are by many. Since rejection was a huge issue in my life, these were difficult years with trying to be or feel accepted.

I felt that there was so much difference between us that this friendship would be short lived, anyhow. But, God had other plans. We were so different in the world's eyes. I lived from paycheck to paycheck raising four children (often with two jobs) and he lived very comfortably with a beautiful home and a summer home.

About this time, I wrote this:
Look closely at this face, what do you see?
The shell of my spirit
The casing others think is me.
I try so hard to be the best I can be; I exercise and diet
    so the outside is a reflection of my spirit.
But today my spirit is sinking
It's tired and emotional;
So much pride in my children
Such a struggle to keep our heads above water; So much
    chasing to keep up with their worlds; So much frustration
    with paying all loans back.
But, what do I see in the mirror?

I see my cross – a gift from David hanging around my neck.
Claiming this shell God has created
Marking God's territory – easing my pain.
He will guide me;
He will pay all my loans;
He will give me the energy to go on and on;
There will be future struggles and pain;
But He has claimed me and marked me as His own.
My spirit begins to sing; my soul rejoices!
For my Lord is all that matters to me!
Praise you, Jesus!
My heart cries to hold you,
*   my arms almost feel your embrace;*
My smile waits to brush against your cheek,
My eyes yearn to see you up close.
As my lips call out David's name and wait tenderly for his
*   lips;*
I feel the pang and have to face reality. You are not here – and
*   I don't know if you ever will be.*
For I have to live for today and enjoy this moment – God is
*   good and satisfies my needs;*
I must keep my mind on Him and me – on my life.
You are just a friend.
So, what do I do with this love?

I remember early on in our dating that he mentioned his children wanted roller blades and he had just purchased them. He asked if my children wanted them, also, as they were the latest craze.

"They know better."

"What do you mean?"

"If it's not their birthdays or Christmas, they don't ask for anything. That's not part of our life."

God had blessed him financially and had not blessed me financially. I enjoyed going out to dinner because it cost me less to feed all of us if I had eaten. Sometimes, he would take his daughter shopping and pick out an outfit for me. That was wonderful because I never had new clothes. One of the most difficult things about dating him was going to church with him because the people at his church dressed up each Sunday and I did not have nice clothes.

I had some business clothes but they were not very good. Sometimes I would take a Sunday off from going to his church because I didn't want to repeat my clothes too often in front of everyone. People dressed more casually at the Catholic Church and that fit my wardrobe better. It was wonderful attending his church and meeting his people – he came from a wonderful world I didn't know existed. It was funny to bring him to events in my world because they were new experiences for him, also. I took him to a school fund-raiser. It was a 50s-60s dance night with a local disc jockey, Dick Biondi. He could not get over the fact we served beer at a fund-raiser for a school. At his fund-raisers for schools, alcohol would not be allowed. This was my first experience with someone who wasn't raised to dance. David had not participated in dances and I danced the first dance with all the women, while he joined the men on the border of the dance floor. After this first dance, I walked over to him.

"I can do that," he said.

"Well, let's go," I said, not knowing that this was a BIG step for him.

The song began and he raised one hand in movement and, suddenly, it was grabbed. Dick Biondi's helpers were picking men to bring on stage. I remember the look of puzzlement on David's face as he was led up the stairs to the stage. The music stopped and these men were asked to do some moves up there removing their shirts and were given a free T-shirt to put on. When removing their shirts, David was the only one up there with an undershirt on – this was definitely a blue collar crowd! He wore his new T-shirt home and I remember thinking I would never see him again. I often wondered why he still called, because our worlds were so different. But, God kept him interested in me and me interested in him no matter what the circumstances were. God had a future planned for us. I didn't see the future very brightly, though. I really saw a lot of stumbling blocks in our way. I knew there were people in his circle fixing him up with other single ladies and it was a little intimidating. But, there were so many good times together. We took walks a lot, talked a lot and helped each other out with parenting tips.

I prayed for acceptance of God's plan so I wouldn't envy or wish for things I wasn't given. I worked on thanking God each day and focusing on what I was grateful for in my life.

My children are healthy, we live in a warm, safe home and I feel a lot of love here. Thank you. I have a job that pays well, is close to home and has a lot of variety – thank you. I have parents who love me and brothers and sisters who care – along with many friends – thank you. I have known love and enjoy your world of love and touching with the opposite sex – thank you. I have learned to speak your words at church and constantly hunger to know more of you – thank you. I love your servant David and know that you will take care of me if he is not my "partner" throughout the rest of my life – thank you. I have money for Christmas presents this year and food on my table every night – thank YOU!

Good Morning, My Lord! Thank you for this day, Friday, January 7, 1994 – tonight, David, me and four of the kids are going to see *Joseph* downtown and I am excited. Yes, about the play, but also about being with my love, David. I do feel growth – especially in my trust and belief that no matter where either of us go – we have a solid foundation in our friendship and we do love each other. Only the Lord knows where our love will go or who or what he will put in our paths to test it or shatter it – but I pray that my sincere love for David will continue to grow. I see such a wonderful man in him – a man I respect and love very much. Thank you, Lord.

Thank you for today, January 19, 1994. The cold wave is lifting – the children are home from school again and I notice their growth. My life has become easier – they help with so many things and I am very grateful. Also, I can fall asleep before all of them – they all put themselves to bed even though I prefer to kiss them good night in their beds. Anyway, when they stay up later than I do, I realize how much they have grown and I realize that a lot of my work has become easier – I can even go home and sleep if I need to – it has been many years of a lot of necessary responsibility and I thank you for the stage my children are at and for my life. You have given me so much – may I always be grateful instead of looking for something else. What you have given me is enough – more than enough – thank you, Lord. I love you and praise your magnificence. Thank you, Lord, for all you have done for me and given me – you have blessed me unbelievably. May I bring others to know you in order for your work to continue on Earth – but also because I love others and wish them to know eternal bliss with you. My life is in your hands – my heart belongs to YOU.

I respected him and it was a wonderful friendship. As time went by, his ex-wife got sicker into alcoholism and when she was put on prescription medication from a dentist, it complicated things and she passed away. She died in her early forties. When you are divorced to an addicted spouse, there is constant tension concerning visitation. That tension was now gone, but so much pain remained for David and his children from her loss.

BUT THE EYES OF THE LORD ARE ON THOSE WHO FEAR HIM, ON THOSE WHOSE HOPE IS IN HIS UNFAILING LOVE. — PSALM 33:18

TEN

Drawn To Each Other

David and I started to date more regularly. Our love continued to grow for each other and we were becoming best friends.

Even though neither of us were ready for marriage yet, we were drawn to each other and it was a battle not to allow ourselves to be drawn physically toward each other over the years of our friendship. We found it was easiest if we went out and went directly home afterward and didn't spend too much time alone together.

In my instance, my love with David seemed more powerful than my love in my first marriage because I felt I knew him better thanks to the honesty in our relationship. It was very difficult to not desire him physically. It was on my mind a lot.

After two years of seeing each other, I decided I needed some time off.

My love for him had grown so strong and I believed it was too strong for a man who was not my husband.

I wrote the following, planning on sending it to a spiritual advisor.

When I really listen to God, I know that nothing else matters except my love for God and my desire to please Him with my life. There is nothing that makes me happier than to believe I am doing what He would want me to do and trusting His Spirit to guide me in my daily choices. I am happy raising my children and praising Him daily. His blessing of David's friendship and love is a benefit, but He is my life. And, please don't think that I take lightly what a wonderful man David is – what a truly blessed friend he has always been and how my love for him continues to grow – sometimes I am awed at how much he has taught me about real love.

Anyway, the dilemma is: The Bible says it is better to marry than burn with passion. And, the story of the woman at the well, when Jesus says "The man you are living with is not your husband either" cuts me deeply. David is not ready for marriage and as my love for him grows; my passion becomes harder to keep from my thoughts. I used to ask God to take this cross from me – let me just accept our friendship as it is and not want to express my love in a physical way – but it sincerely comes down to the fact that David is currently the major issue in my life that invites me to sin – isn't that crazy? That love can create a sinful nature by wanting physical expression and I am dating someone who does not want to marry?

If I stop dating David, I will truly lose a real love – but if I continue, I am setting myself up with wrongful desires for him.

Every month I go through this thought pattern. I try to give myself a realistic deadline of how long I will wait (and then I think of the Bible passage that says Love is Patient and feel impatient).

Should I stop seeing him?

I felt we were dedicated to each other, yet I knew he was not ready for a second marriage. But physically, I desired him intensely. So, I scheduled a dinner and had prepared him that I needed to speak about *us*. I wanted to speak to him about stepping back from the relationship and have us calm down our feelings for each other. By this time, I had been divorced and a single parent for over eight years, he had only been a single parent for three. That was a big difference. I knew we were at different points in being ready for remarriage and I needed to back off. So, as I anticipated this talk, I cried all day.

We went out for a nice dinner on October 8, 1994 and I spoke for over an hour about how I understood that we were at different places in our life. I spoke about how much I loved him yet needed to step back because my feelings were too strong for dating. I spoke about so many things as he quietly sat and listened. By the end of dinner, I gave him his turn. I asked him what he thought about our relationship and asked if he agreed with me. He looked at me for a minute and pulled a ring out of his pocket.

"I think we should get married," he said matter-of-factly.

My shock seemed to be felt throughout the restaurant. We were both sitting in silence; me staring at the ring on the table and David staring at my expression as our waitress approached the table.

"Oh, is this an engagement?!" she asked.

I couldn't say a word. A very unusual thing! I stared at the ring and then at him – smiling broadly – and back at the ring. What a night and what an amazing, comical man! He had asked all four of my children's permission earlier that day, so they had seen me cry all day knowing he was going to propose.

We planned a wedding for the next summer, July 8th of 1995. We knew we were going to join two families – my four teenagers and his two teenagers under one roof – but what a wonderful love we shared and we dove into this marriage in love and ready to deal with whatever life brought the two of us.

While engaged, David took me to a home being built on Poplar Avenue in Elmhurst. It was property that originally had a smaller home that was torn down and a larger home was being built on the lot. Walking from room to room, it was difficult for me to *see* the rooms and space we would have, but we both fell in love with it as home. For me, anything was better than my small condo and this home could fit four of my condos in it. David asked my opinion on the color of the tubs.

"As long as they are not purple," I replied. Our tub in the condo had been a light shade of purple.

The children came to look at our new home site and Brian looked cautiously at David.

"Will the driveway have a slope?" he asked.

"Why do you ask, Bri?" David responded.

"I was wondering if it could be flat to play basketball."

"I'll be sure it's perfect for a basketball net Bri," David said smiling.

I later explained to David the tears in my eyes. Brian, after giving up playing basketball at home to God years ago, was hearing God, through David, provide his heart's desire.

MAY HE GIVE YOU THE DESIRE OF YOUR HEART. — PSALM 20:4

I felt like Cinderella moving into a castle when I moved into this home a month before our wedding. It was a magnificent home and each room was prettier than the next. I had never really visited homes this size, let alone live in one. My furniture did not move with us, (of course, my couch with a leg missing would have been out of place) but David slowly filled the home with furniture. My uncle stopped by with my mom and asked when the restaurant opened. He had never seen a home with such a large kitchen.

Father, how do I begin to thank you for the future you extend to me – how do I thank you for a wonderful man to love – compassionate, thoughtful, insightful, loving, funny, generous, understanding – are just a few of his qualities. And how do I thank you for a new home – a home like heaven itself – with room for all our children, beautiful windows, warmth, a fireplace and master bedroom/bathroom that is so gorgeous. I marvel at the wonder of it all – marvel at picking out light fixtures and staircases when I have spent years of having a difficult time feeding my children. How can these two opposite worlds relate? Only in your awesomeness – only in your marvelousness – it is only through you that I can begin to imagine and enjoy life without want and desire – you prepare a place for me and continue to work wonders for me here on earth. I praise you, Lord – Can I praise you enough? Never! For if I praise you for thousands of years that will not be enough for your generosity toward me, a sinner. Father, may I learn more about you and praise you more and more – may I please you everyday, in everything I do and say.

The night before our wedding, David's daughter Erika moved in as she planned on staying with my four children while we were on our honeymoon. His son Nathan was in a boarding school for behavior modification.

Friday evening, July 7th, as David and I walked around the home, anticipating our wedding the next day, we heard screaming. Erika and Ellen were shouting at each other. David got upset. I felt like my Cinderella dream had just evaporated. I really didn't know if he would show up the next day for our wedding. I wouldn't blame him if he didn't want to handle more teenagers than the two lives he was already trying desperately to salvage from the destructive loss of his first marriage.

I awoke the next morning and walked around slowly – slowly putting things together for a possible wedding that afternoon. Around 9:00 am, I heard his voice in the kitchen and my heart leaped for joy. He was still going to marry me even though our home life really looked difficult.

The wedding was wonderful. We celebrated God and His plan in both of our lives that had allowed us to experience a new opportunity for love. We chose to speak at the ceremony, thanking all in attendance for their love and support. One of my favorite lines was from David to our friends and family who were present.

"You have given us love when we felt unloved."

IF YOU HAVE ANY ENCOURAGEMENT FROM BEING UNITED WITH CHRIST, IF ANY COMFORT FROM HIS LOVE, IF ANY FELLOWSHIP WITH THE SPIRIT, IF ANY TENDERNESS AND COMPASSION, THEN MAKE MY JOY COMPLETE BY BEING LIKE-MINDED, HAVING THE SAME LOVE, BEING ONE IN SPIRIT AND PURPOSE. — PHILIPPIANS 2:1-2

One song that was sung, *Only God Could Love You More*, had

lyrics that expressed our love to all those that God had used to walk alongside us through difficult seasons. And now, they chose to watch God's culmination of a wonderful new union.

It was a very hot July and we went to Galena to golf for our honeymoon. One day, we decided to take a boat ride to relax and, since it was air-conditioned, thought it would be an enjoyable cruise. It turned out to be a gambling boat that never really made it to the Mississippi. We laughed at our efforts and really enjoyed each other. I knew I was in love with a wonderful man and anticipated growing old with him.

My ex-husband struggled to contact the children after I left the marriage. I set up visitations, but because of his lack of involvement in their lives, by the time I married David, my children did not have a relationship with their birth father. They watched David curiously for the first few years. Our home was a trial ground – it was as if the parents were trying to convince the teenagers that they had value – that they were loved and accepted. David was very good at accepting people. He could even be nice to telephone solicitors during dinner.

He seemed to make everyone feel good that they talked to him. He treated everyone with value. So, it didn't surprise me that after being married a couple of years, our college girls asked David to adopt them. We stood before a judge and heard him tell the girls that anyone can be a father and give genes to children, but it took someone special to be called your dad. What an amazing gift. Going from a male parent figure that didn't have any time for you to a man who looked for reasons to do something for you, spend time with you, encourage you. They officially became his daughters and were thrilled to call him dad.

My boys were away at school a lot but once they spent some time with David, they, too, desired to be adopted by him.

David wanted the boys to know boy things – like things a mom wouldn't think to teach them. So, one Christmas Eve he gave them Swiss army knives. Kevin walked down the stairs on Christmas morning with a band-aid on seven out of ten of his fingers.

"Guess which Christmas present I was playing with last night?" he asked.

David roared. He loved it and I think that memory became his very favorite Christmas present memory. He spoke about it often.

GOD IS NOT UNJUST; HE WILL NOT FORGET YOUR WORK AND THE LOVE YOU HAVE SHOWN HIM AS YOU HAVE HELPED HIS PEOPLE AND CONTINUE TO HELP THEM. WE WANT EACH OF YOU TO SHOW THIS SAME DILIGENCE TO THE VERY END, IN ORDER TO MAKE YOUR HOPE SURE. — HEBREWS 6:10-11

ELEVEN

As Best We Could

When we married, David had said that I didn't have to work. I couldn't quite process that information. I had worked, earning income, most of my life. And, since being a single mom, I had often had two jobs at the same time. Not work? How could this be? So, I agreed to work part-time instead of full-time. I applied and got a job in the business office of a Christian school. It was fun learning more about this school community because it was part of the community my husband was raised in.

It was very different from the community I was raised in because men were leaders. Besides priests, most men were quiet in my world, prior to David. In fact, I remember the first time I was at David's church and all the elders walked up to give out communion. They were in suits and it was a holy moment for me because I experienced the feeling of being under a *covering* of these men.

I had never enjoyed the covering before and this made an impression on me. These men were trying to walk closely with God and serve His people. It was magical for me to see so many men I could respect.

While we had dated, I would attend the Catholic church on a Sunday morning with my children and the Christian Reformed church later that morning with him and his children. This continued throughout the first years of our marriage. I learned so much about the similarities of these churches. One great gift from a class at his church called *Understanding Your Spiritual Gifts* was that I was told I had a gift of intercession. I remember asking the pastor what that meant.

"Do you like to pray?" he asked.

"Sure."

But, as a Catholic, I confess I mostly knew the rosary prayers. He suggested I study prayer because God had gifted me in it. It was like a parent seeing a child draw and encouraging them to study their artistic talent. I dove into prayer books and classes. This became a step that changed my life. I was, indeed, a prayer warrior and the more I learned, the more I wanted to spend time in prayer.

At this Christian school, I remember learning about Christian education and how Biblical teaching may differ a little from Catholic teaching. I worked on computers and substituted when some of the secretaries in the school offices were out sick or on vacation. It was a wonderful job, especially because I worked alongside two wonderful women and respected the two men in authority over us.

It also helped me to see my stepdaughter while working there – I had hoped to be a good *motherly* influence in her life. I never expected to replace her mom, but did hope to show her a mother's love and how it could bless her life.

I learned about *Moms In Touch*. It was a group of moms who met once a week to pray for the school and their children. This group taught me how to pray using Scripture verses and I loved it. I started a *Moms In Touch* group at my sons' school, but continued to work at Erika's school.

Nathan had gone her school also, but was gone from there by the time I was employed. After several years of working there, David and I decided I could donate my time instead of working for a paycheck and I left to pursue volunteering at a Walk In Ministry.

Cleaning our home, making meals and working with all the teenagers was especially challenging, but I remember many sweet afternoons with fresh cookies out of the oven when the teenagers came home from school. I continued to study prayer during those years and my schooling encouraged my walk with Christ and healing for others and myself.

David and I would go away once in a while – just to nurture our relationship. We would let the children, since they ranged in age from 14-21, take care of the home as we stayed overnight at a hotel with a golf course. We had great relaxation times and were able to be refreshed to balance our lives.

One evening, we had just checked into our hotel room, started to unpack a few things and the phone rang. It was the police – Nathan had run away, again, from where he was being helped. We needed to work this out before decompressing.

His mental illness seemed to convince him, once he was on his meds, that he didn't need medication or treatment. He felt "normal" because of the prescriptions, but upon feeling normal, would run away from anywhere that tried to help him. I admit that some of the places in Illinois were just holding places where it was difficult for a young man to want to stay, and where there was no fun in life, but he was kept sane in these places.

Our teenagers at home had struggled through those difficult years, including experimenting with alcohol. We came home from one weekend to see the home spotless. We knew someone had cleaned up. When we saw that there was not one piece of garbage in our cans, we confronted the children. It wasn't even garbage day yet. Ellen admitted to having had a party – caught because she had cleaned up too well!

Every spring, David and I would become bleacher parents and we loved it. My boys played high school baseball and both of my girls played high school softball. Ellen even played in college. I really missed sitting on the bench cheering them on when those years ended.

One of my favorite places to be is outside on a spring day watching someone I love play ball. The smell of fresh air, the feel of the good earth beneath your sneakers, the laughter of children at play, comfy seat cushions to ease the length of the game on your rear end and good conversation with other parents, coupled with cheering on and encouraging your child every time they were up to bat or the ball came near them – oh – those were fun times.

Each of our children had psychological consequences by having been raised by someone who deserted them. Yes, we can blame the disease and say they were a "good person, just sick." That's fine. But the sickness still took away their ability to parent and show love and acceptance to their children. The sickness still caused rejection and each of our children had to deal with that – along with dealing with a new person their remaining parent loved.

We had boundaries laid out beforehand for all the children but, still, there were numerous occasions that David and I had both wondered if our getting married was the right thing to do. Not questioning, at all, our union and our love for each other, but questioning if our marriage was the *right*, healthiest thing to do for these teenagers. The reason that we believed that it still was, even though there had been difficult times, was because we believed that the life that would come out of that union and the love that would come out of that union was a great gift that we could give our children. We knew their first choice was not another parent in their life.

One of the largest challenges was working with Nathan who was dealing with drugs as a teenager. He had broken a contract he had with David, prior to our marriage, that if he used drugs again, he would have to go to a special school. He knew he was out of control and agreed to go.

With the help of a psychologist, David found a school in Indiana and it was a wonderful place for behavior modification. His time at that school allowed him to get his high school diploma. He did not live with us the first year and a half of our marriage, but when they wanted him to try some college classes we brought him home to live with us.

After a few months of total chaos living with him, through visits to counselors, he was diagnosed with schizophrenia. So, this behavior modification school, even though it served some purpose in his life, did not help his mental condition. Because of this mental disorder, he couldn't be modified behaviorally. There was too much going on psychologically.

When he came to live with us in December 1996, we had been married one and a half years. January, February and March of 1997 were some of the most difficult months of our marriage because his behavior was so outrageous.

Nathan was a man in chaos. He was not listening to any of our boundaries; he would not follow any home guidelines. He dyed his hair green (and made quite a mess in the bathroom and laundry with green dye), shaved his head so severely it was bleeding, tore up a book and stapled each page individually to his wall, left in the middle of the night leaving our house doors open, and much more bizarre behavior.

There was so much going on mentally, as we understood later, but during this time we found out he was on drugs. We gave him a choice to get help or move out. We needed to reinforce our home rules with the other teenagers watching all of this.

He decided to drive to Washington state to visit a friend. Somehow he got there and called us agreeing to go into a program. Well, we put him in a drug rehab program to find out that his marijuana use was not as severe as they needed it to be. They would not help us.

Trying to get him into help with a mental institution was difficult. They have so many guidelines and he was not meeting all of them. He was not threatening his own or other's lives (so they said). We finally found a program in a nearby town and they helped us get him on Risperdal, which helped him with his schizophrenia. Over the months this took, our lives were chaotic. His mental state was bizarre.

This touched on our 12-step education. Each day, we could only do the best we could and try to help him stay alive. Dealing with a mental disorder was even more difficult than dealing with alcoholism or drug addictions, in our opinion. The behavior may be similar but people struggling with drugs and alcohol still make a choice.

Nathan wasn't able to make a choice because his mind and the mental disorder were not allowing him to have choices. He was simply trying to live with the non-reality that was going on in his head. Once he was on medication, we gave him some time to get settled. We supported him in an apartment as long as he stayed on his medication.

Unfortunately, once medicated, he believed he was just like everyone else and would go off of it. Within weeks of going off, he would search for street drugs to quiet the chaos in his mind. It was a vicious cycle that led us through painful years of struggles for sanity in our home.

We visited him at more places in Illinois for the mentally ill than I knew a state could have. Most of them housed mentally ill and elderly – which was especially sad to see. So many elderly people, left to sit all day in a wheelchair in the hallways – waiting, hoping for someone to talk to them.

Erika, in spite of many counseling sessions, chose comfort from her pain in ways that created tension in her life and in our relationship. As parents, we sought counseling centers and learned that she would go for a time, but since it was our desire for her to get help and not hers, we didn't see healing in her pain through the programs.

We had to spend time studying our codependent lessons and let her choices have natural consequences.

We always told our children that our love was unconditional but relationships were conditional. They had to do their part to be in relationship with us. It is difficult to wait for hurt children to do their part in relating. But, the Lord helped us. He reminded us of books that gave insight in creating healthy boundaries in our family.

FOR EVERYTHING THAT WAS WRITTEN IN THE PAST WAS WRITTEN TO TEACH US, SO THAT THROUGH ENDURANCE AND THE ENCOURAGEMENT OF THE SCRIPTURES WE MIGHT HAVE HOPE. — ROMANS 15:4

TWELVE

A Gift of Time

While dealing with the children's issues, David's family business sold. His dad had started the business. Looking back and talking about it in 2008, he said it was God's perfect timing for the business to sell.

MANY ARE THE PLANS IN A MAN'S HEART, BUT IT IS THE LORD'S PURPOSE THAT PREVAILS. — PROVERBS 19:21

At the time, however, it was very painful for him, as he loved his work and the fellowship he had with each employee. His business was more of a ministry than a business to him. After selling, he tried to work with the new owners, but that lasted less than a year, as he didn't like how this company was treating his former employees.

So, David became a full time partner with me. It was quite an adjustment for both of us. I was used to having my own time and all of a sudden, he was asking where I was going. And, for him, he tried hard to swallow this new role which was a little sour in his mouth. Finally, six months into it, we sat at dinner at his favorite restaurant in Elmhurst.

"I need to know what you are feeling, honey," I pleaded.

"I hate getting up in the morning with nowhere to go," he answered with a mist appearing in his eyes.

His dad had gone to "the office/garage" every morning, Monday through Saturday, for coffee and conversation. David expected to do the same until he was 80. When he expressed it out loud it gave me some grace to hear his battle. So, we decided, he just needed a new routine. He began making coffee at home, going to his home office and reading the newspaper on the Internet. This routine took about an hour because some of the time was spent with the Bible. Then, he was ready to see what God wanted him to do that day. It became a wonderful life filled with many exciting days. God had given him many open choices and the gift of time.

His parents had a small place in Florida and we began spending more time in the warmer climate. What a blessing not to have to deal with Chicago all winter! If we were going to stay longer than a week, we tried to drive. During those 20-hour drives, we learned a lot about each other – we even learned many things we didn't need to know.

I continued to study prayer. I also enjoyed what I had learned through books like *Me and My Big Mouth*. I purchased it as a joke when I saw the title and gave it to David to give to me at Christmas, so the children could laugh. After it sat on my shelf for a while, the Holy Spirit nudged me to read it. To date, I have read it over five times because it takes time for some things to sink in with me – and my words are so very plentiful that it is taking God some time to *season* them. "Our strengths are also our weaknesses" – one of David's favorite quotes. My strength of liking to talk is a weakness when I share too much and too often.

The teenagers' issues took front row for quite a while in our marriage. After several years of trying to understand Nathan's mental illness, we heard of a program at a hospital – a trial program for a new drug for schizophrenia. He qualified and we hoped for new medications to give him a better life. After one week in this new program, he attacked David.

The next visit, David went in without me, and came out very upset. He said his son was sitting in a corner of the room scratching his body, uncommunicative. David immediately took him out of the program and they divulged that he had been given a placebo. We knew there was a chance of that, but we had hoped for the new medication to really help him.

Seeing him with no medication – with that placebo or sugar pill – showed us how truly ill our son was. We were devastated and worked harder to keep him safe from himself – to do all we could to keep him on medication.

In 2000, we were called by the adoption agency. Nathan's birth father wanted to meet him. He lived in Denver and wanted him to come there. Nathan, when stable on his meds, was very excited about this.

We checked things out as best we could, and being an adult, he went to meet his birth father. His birth father helped him get settled in the Denver mental health system, so he stayed on his medications there. They both asked if he could permanently live there and not return to Illinois.

This turned out to be a great blessing. He had much more freedom than he had in Illinois and loved the climate. He would have field trips to the mountains and freedom to walk around town, some things he never got to experience in Illinois. We talked to him weekly and visited him in Denver when possible. His move to Denver gave us a little more time to spend on the other children.

They all had some issues but, don't we all? Ellen's knee was injured in softball and she had arthroscopic surgery in high school. Now, she was playing college softball and the team flew to Florida for a tournament. David and I flew there to support her and, after finding the field, saw Ellen limp up to us on crutches. She had re-injured the same knee in practice. So, we spent time with her in Florida on the bench – and enjoyed spending time cheering on her team.

But, I remember David wondering if we had made the right decision as parents – to spend money flying to watch a tournament that our child didn't play in. Decisions as parents – always making the best decision you can with the knowledge you have that day – and always wishing for more knowledge!

After Florida, her teeth started hurting and after examination by dentists, it was determined that she needed jaw surgery. She had fallen from the top bunk in college onto a table and injured her jaw. The surgery included a year of braces prior to surgery, plates, screws, her mouth wired shut for six weeks and more braces. This was a very difficult time for her and us.

As I watched her the afternoon after surgery, she vomited. Now, with your mouth wired shut, this is very dangerous. I decided to stay the night and by the third or fourth vomiting episode, 11 hours after surgery and in the middle of the night, I called the nurses to get the head nurse. The head nurse was not happy with me for calling her, but no doctor was on the floor. Since Ellen was on medication to stop vomiting and was not stopping, I asked the head nurse if the tube in her throat could possibly be causing the vomiting. The nurse spoke about the tube being a double-edged sword – it may cause vomiting, but it was also necessary to pump blood out of her stomach. I took the responsibility for any blood in her stomach and asked them to remove it. She slept for hours after it was removed and never vomited again. We both slept well.

Then, six weeks of blending any food until it became liquid – she would sit at the table with us, but her mashed potatoes and gravy in the blender just didn't quite seem like the mashed potatoes and gravy we were consuming. I fed her for a while, until she got the hang of inserting a tube through the hole between her molar and wisdom tooth and using a long syringe to draw the liquid out of a glass into the tube and down her throat. She lost a lot of weight and we were concerned. Plus her emotional attitude was definitely tested and quite strained. I can't begin to understand all she felt during these months.

Other family members were moving on to other adventures. Kevin chose Illinois State University for college and worked hard at partying. He was brilliant and usually bored in classes, but the partying quickly got his attention. He was not allowed back the next year and chose jobs for several years that did not promise him a future. He worked hard at many things, but for $10-$12 an hour.

Brian chose Valparaiso University in Indiana. With a friend for a roommate and a degree in Sports Management offered, it was the school for him. He excelled in college.

David parented all four of the children I brought into the marriage through college and wrapped his fatherly arms around them. He loved them like God, the Father, does and showed them a sincere father's heart.

The years of raising six teenagers together were taking a toll on us, but our marriage stayed strong. We loved life and searched for any moments of joy we could uncover. These were usually found on the golf course. We both enjoyed the sport and David was great at seeing something in anyone's swing and correcting it for a better game.

While worshiping one evening at church, thoughts started vibrating through my brain about celebrating David's life. He never wanted a birthday party, but I planned a surprise party in June of 2001, just after his birthday. I told him I needed him to look at a golf picture at a pro shop (where I had rented the dining hall). He was so frustrated with me for making him stop at this pro shop on our way to dinner that he didn't even notice he parked right next to our daughter's convertible. Many people from his past were able to attend. We had a wonderful time celebrating all God had made of his life since 1990, when he was at a low point after losing his first wife.

In 2002, I arrived home from a weekend retreat to greet a very joyful David. He was excited because on one of his adventurous walks (he loved to walk through construction sites) he purchased two condominiums in a new construction project downtown. He thought it was such a good investment, he wanted one for us to downsize into and one for resale. I asked him to consider just the one we would live in, since it sounded like a gamble to me. He did. He acted like my opinion mattered, even though I had about less than one percent of the business sense and experience he had. We put our home up for sale and, with everything in order, moved into a very small, cement surrounded home.

The benefits of walking to dinner, banks, the library, and other spots were amazing. But the size, and David having no garage or place to "putz around" caused a very difficult living experience for him.

I remember the day, after only unpacking for about a couple of months, that I saw him pacing back and forth – literally – pacing back and forth like a caged lion – looking, hoping for something to accomplish.

I suggested we move. He agreed. He was a farm boy and felt trapped in such close quarters. City living was not his style, just yet. We found a much larger town home in Darien and he was excited when they accepted our offer.

The next day, during that five-day window in the purchase contract, David had surgery to remove a collection – sort of a lump – of fluid in his neck. The surgery went well, but even better was what the Lord did with it.

As I saw David being wheeled away to the operating room, in that flimsy hospital gown, slippers and plastic cap, I heard the clear voice of the Lord in a thought.

"David belongs on a golf course."

I ran outside during his surgery and called our niece, who was our realtor.

"We need to stop the deal on the town home and find a home on a golf course." I said to her.

"Aunt Mary, let's wait until after surgery and you are a little less emotional," she replied.

"Okay," I said.

As soon as David awoke in recovery I raised the subject.

"Honey, you always said that someday you would like to live on a golf course. Neither of us knows how many days the Lord has planned for us. Why wait for someday? Why not try it and if it doesn't work, we can move to the town home?"

"No argument here," he said, smiling gently.

After he arrived home, we began making plans. He mentioned that the only golf course he had ever played that he would never tire of was in a far west suburb . So, we called a friend who worked in that area and she helped us find a home on the course. Our backyard became a sand trap and a lot of green grass. David's dream.

Our white frame farmhouse stands on a corner of our small ten acre farm. It has stood there, along with the land, never changing for thirty years, the changing world around it never affected it. Looking east from our porch window one sees the simple beauty of our land. In back of it the rolling green hills of a golf course can be seen. Along side of it the smooth grassy acres of parkland are noticed. In the spring the black fertile land is a picture of refreshment. The summer brings forth green vegetables and green leaves which shade our house from the hot, blistering summer sun. The fall turns the land into a colorful scene. The snow of winter covers the land with a huge white blanket. The land is, year round, a picture of beauty. Its murmuring brook, with its rustic, old bridge and the reflection of a full moon shimmering on its water, its variety of flowers, its plentiful, assorted supply of animal life, its odd atmosphere of "oldness" in contrast to its modern surroundings, the simplicity of it being "just" farmland – these have painted an everlasting picture of beauty and serenity in my mind. — Dave Bulthuis, English 103B (1964)

I remember driving to the home with our belongings. He was a little concerned in the car.

"I've never done this before – left everyone I know – my connections for air conditioning, plumbing, everything around the home."

I assured him that the new area had capable people for him to hire. But, now I realize that what he meant was – well, you see – David was a creature of habit. He golfed with the same foursome on a trip for 30 years. He had coffee at the same time each morning. He always had something cold with his hot dinner. He had ice cream with chocolate sauce every night before bed. He switched that years later to two chocolate chip cookies and milk, but even if we were out of town, he needed the same thing to eat before bed. He liked repetition. He felt, moving out west, that he had lost a lot of his routine. It was definitely a step of faith for him to pick up and move 30 miles west.

The second day in the home, I remember walking into the garage as he was unpacking.

"Honey, what do you think?" I asked.

"My next step is heaven," he answered.

We had a wonderful couples' small group at our church our entire marriage and really enjoyed relating as a couple. We socialized with new couples through the golf community. We had so much fun golfing we began getting involved in couples' events and met wonderful neighbors and friends.

We had so much fun golfing. They had so many events and we both enjoyed golf and the people. We often skipped down the fairway, if we were walking. David would dance on the tee box if he liked his drive. Even though some of our children continued to struggle, joy was abundant in our lives.

Two weeks after moving, our daughter Erin and her husband Donny found out they were expecting their first child. I measured out the mileage in the car from our new home to their town home and was excited to see we lived exactly two miles from them. That was a distance I could deal with for my grandchildren's home!!

On a Monday in December we spent the day in the hospital waiting room playing cards. It was Erin's 29th birthday. When Donny came walking out crying, we all held our breath for the news, hoping it was good. He was so moved by the birth it took him a while to ask us all into the room to meet his family and he wouldn't tell us the sex. He wanted mom to tell us. As we entered the room, she shouted excitedly, "It's a girl!" Macy's name came from Uncle Kevin at the Thanksgiving table. As we sat around trying to combine grandparent's names for our new family member, Kevin said, Macy – MA from Mary and CY from Nancy – since the two grandmothers were Mary and Nancy. As soon as we all heard it, we all loved it. And, thankfully, Erin and Donny loved it too.

Grandparenting is a whole new world. We couldn't play enough. We didn't know we had that much love to give. We thought of her in every store and at every turn. It was difficult to spend time in Florida, even though it was David's favorite pastime when snow began to fall. We would go to Florida for two weeks and back here to spend a week with her. David asked our children to have any more grandbabies in the spring, when we knew we could handle Chicago weather for at least six months!

In 2005, while holding a job with a mortgage finance company, Kevin found out he was gifted with numbers.

"I keep hearing – go back to school – but I can't," he said.

"Why not?" David asked.

"Because I have to work full time to pay all of my bills."

"If you go back to school and get As and Bs, while keeping a part-time job, I will help you financially pay for school."

David then looked at me and tilted his head toward our bedroom – his sign for me to go to the other room to talk. I did and waited. My insides were jumping.

"Okay," he said gently, "I know you are excited. You need to keep quiet and let him decide if he wants to do this."

"Do you know how great it will be if he goes back to school and gets a degree?"

"Of course I do, but we need to let him learn that. It doesn't matter if we want it for him. He has to want it for himself."

Parenting. Sometimes so complicated. I stayed quiet and our son went back to school. He found out he *was* good with numbers and graduated three years later with a degree in Accounting.

David's parents had purchased a small efficiency condo in the 1980s in Pompano Beach, Florida. It was a very small unit, but had a magnificent view of a lighthouse and the ocean. It was on an inlet and you could watch the boats come in and out from either entertaining or catching fish. Beautiful boats of all sizes and colors. Some with sails and many with loud motors, which I think they call cigarette boats. They watched and enjoyed people having fun with water, caught their own shrimp and visited with relatives who purchased units in the same complex.

His mom was wheelchair bound and it blessed her to spend time in warmer weather during the winter. When they passed away, David asked to purchase the unit. Once his business sold, however, and he had more time to spend there, the smallness of this old-efficiency-hotel-room-turned-into-a-condo shrunk around his large frame. He bumped his knee trying to shave in the tiny bathroom – twisting and turning to get in a comfortable position.

"I need more room!" he hollered one evening.

I laughed. He was a tall man and it was difficult for him to move around in the bathroom. I sat in the bathroom to read at night, while he watched TV in the main room, so I agreed.

David loved exploring. So, we began exploring the region, searching for more room. We finally gave up because the rising costs and unavailability of views of the ocean in our price range exhausted us. Then, one sunny day on the golf course, they put a man with us who asked where we lived.

"We are in Pompano Beach in a small unit. We tried looking for a two bedroom, but gave up. We are leaving it up to God, now."

"My building has some two bedroom units for sale. I'll help God," he answered.

We stopped by his building with him on the way home and didn't like the two units available. As we were leaving, the secretary said someone on the fourth floor was thinking of selling. We knocked on the door and met a young family. They gave us the number of their father-in-law in Indiana. We were amazed as soon as we walked inside. It was old and needed work, but the view was breathtaking.

All ocean, sand and beach front as far as you could see to the south, as it was an end unit with south and east views, and sliding glass doors for windows. Beach front to the north all the way to the beautiful lighthouse David and his parents had looked at for years in the efficiency unit. We spent nine months renovating it, sold the efficiency unit and began spending time in a "little slice of heaven," Silver Thatch Ocean Club.

Good Morning, Lord. It's Monday, October 28, 2002 – I'm watching You peak over the clouds at 6:45 am. You are casting a beautiful hue below Your cloud – a color I can't describe – as You dance in and out of the billows – shining light where You choose – making some of the cloud sparkle while other parts sit and watch You explode. You are dazzling – Your brilliance cannot be hidden much longer – no cloud can hold You back – You are magnificent, Lord – I look forward to spending this day with You. I love you, Mary

PS – Your waves make noise this morning. They dance toward shore and break in constant ripples flowing with Your wind. They kiss the shore gently and pull back in humility – lest they come closer than You allow. Their blue-green hues dance toward our sight and just as we capture their beauty they crest into Your white bubbles.

This was our wonderful gift from God to use when it was cold in Chicago.

Each season in Florida, "Davy Crockett" (as I called him sometimes) and I continued to explore. He would find a golf course community on the west side of Florida and we would participate in a stay and play package. We visited many wonderful communities in the hopes of finding one that would become our Florida home when we were older. He hoped we'd become snowbirds living on a Florida golf course some day.

In 2006, we found it. It was called Heron Creek, located in North Port, Florida. We both loved it immediately. We felt right at home and found the course enjoyable. David visited in December of 2006 and made a bid on a home! He knew the floor plan we both liked and, when I got to see it that winter, I knew it was the most wonderful home I had ever known. Even though it was a year old, it had never been lived in so we began furnishing it.

We put our unit up for sale in Pompano Beach and turned our finances over to the Lord. One day we were driving across Alligator Alley, from Pompano to North Port and David mentioned that he might need to do something new with the Pompano realtor.

"After all," he said, "I haven't heard much and we need to sell that unit."

I reminded him that he had turned it over to God to handle and he didn't need to do anything. He smiled and decided to let any thoughts of concern over its sale go. Two hours later we got a call and were faxed an offer on the unit. It was amazing to watch his face as he received the offer. He was enjoying God handling it!

THEREFORE DO NOT WORRY ABOUT TOMORROW, FOR TOMORROW WILL WORRY ABOUT ITSELF. — MATTHEW 6:34

We furnished our new home and in the fall of 2007, really felt at home in Florida. We invited friends to stay with us – it was the first time we had room for anyone else – and really enjoyed being snowbirds. David would often say that he couldn't have imagined a better day – warm weather, a game of golf with his wife, relaxing in a pool afterward, followed by a nice dinner.

It was the life he had always dreamed of and he was living it.

→ ψ ←

WE WAIT IN HOPE FOR THE LORD; HE IS OUR HELP AND OUR SHIELD. IN HIM OUR HEARTS REJOICE, FOR WE TRUST IN HIS HOLY NAME. MAY YOUR UNFAILING LOVE REST UPON US, O LORD, EVEN AS WE PUT OUR HOPE IN YOU. — PSALM 33:20-22

Thirteen

Hon, We Have A Problem

He called it a little discomfort on his right side. We golfed that day and had a tee time for the following day because we were returning to Chicago that week.

"It's probably a pulled muscle," I reassured him.

"I don't know if I want to golf tomorrow," he said.

"Honey, if you don't know if you want to golf, we need to see a doctor."

He golfed the next day and standing in the kitchen, right after our round, he spoke "I'm golfed out."

"What?!" I exclaimed. "You, golfed out?"

He smiled. "I'm ready to go back to Chicago," he said.

But, he *was* golfed out. We just didn't know.

He left for his doctor appointment on Good Friday, March 21st, while I left for a hair appointment. Leaving the salon, I pulled my car over in the parking lot because my cell phone rang.

"How was your visit?" I asked.

"Hon, we have a problem – or at least I do," he said.

"Honey, if you have a problem, we have a problem. What is it?" I replied.

"They found some fluid below my right lung, where there shouldn't be fluid. I have an appointment on Monday with a pulmonary doctor."

"Okay – we'll deal with it on Monday." I replied.

"Yeah," he said.

Easter weekend was nice with a brunch with the family at the club. He seemed a little tired on Sunday. We met Dr. Yu on Monday and he showed us the test results and what they meant to him.

"This fluid looks like the results of an untreated infection, like pneumonia. It would be similar to the mess a hurricane would leave on land. Some untreated infection left a mess for us to clean up. I can drain it as soon as Wednesday. It's an outpatient procedure called a thoracentesis."

"Okay," we said, "sign us up for Wednesday."

"Most people feel much better once the fluid is removed and it usually only takes one removal."

"What are the chances it could be fluid from cancer?" David asked.

"Could a tumor cause this? Yes, it could and we can't tell because the fluid is hiding the area. But, the chances of it being cancer are about 20 percent."

We drove home expecting a procedure on Wednesday that would take care of this fluid buildup.

While he was getting prepared for the removal of the fluid, we had quite a wait. The doctor had been double booked. David teased the nurses by pretending to dance out of the room twice. We all laughed at his inability to wait – especially in a hospital gown. Once the doctor came, we spoke about Darrell Stremler, a close friend of ours who had established the medical practice many years before. The doctor called him an amazing man. David added that, he David, was amazing. I quickly corrected him.

"You are not amazing – Jesus in you is amazing, though!"

We all chuckled.

I had to leave the room and when I returned, there lay a huge bag of fluid.

"Look at that," said Dr. Yu.

"Holy Smokers!" I exclaimed.

It was quite large – filled with a yellow fluid with pink/reddish speckles swirling around.

"He handled it like a champ!" said Dr. Yu.

They took him for a lung X-ray immediately afterward. I waited and when they returned, David was white – they made him lay down and brought things to revive him – his blood pressure had dropped.

"As soon as they asked me to stand for the X-ray, I was okay, but when I had to turn for them, I felt myself going," he said.

The loss of so much fluid may have thrown his equilibrium off.

We drove home, excited to have it over with. We waited for two days for results and during those two days, he seemed to get weaker. He had little appetite and rested. He had a small cough. On Friday, the doctor called at 11:00 AM to say that the preliminary results showed exactly what he expected. He asked me how David was doing.

"Actually, doctor, he is not doing well," I replied.

"Okay, let's put him on antibiotics," he offered. "It may be that the infection is not totally out of his body yet."

"Okay," I said appreciatively.

I drove to the drugstore to pick up the antibiotic and David took it immediately. I was sure he would feel much better fast. At 2:00 PM, the doctor called again. He asked us to both get on the line and asked if we wanted to come into his office to talk.

"No," David said, "what is it?"

"The final results are in and we are shocked," he said. "They found some cancer cells in the fluid."

The conversation continued for several minutes – type of cancer, stage, did we hear him correctly? Our minds started to whirl as we hung up the phone and sat together with tears beginning to form. David looked at me.

"What do I tell Macy?" he said.

"Honey, she will go through this season with us – her PaPa may have a battle to fight, but she will understand."

We phoned the children and asked them to come over. David went online and looked up the term adenocarcinoma.

"The hits just keep on coming," he said.

We read the discouraging news about this nasty disease: ten percent survival rate – well, we decided he was going to be one of the ten percent.

When the children arrived, we told them what we knew and what we didn't know, as the word cancer began to penetrate our brains and emotions.

I sent out prayer requests to two Bible study groups and one sister sent me the information on a web site called Caring Bridge. I set up a page for David, in order to communicate easily to friends and family members. I phoned a brother who recently battled two types of cancer to get his opinion on where to go. Dr. Yu had already contacted one oncologist for us and they had set us up to call on Monday for a PET scan on Tuesday. Then, visiting with the oncologist he recommended on Thursday, as they needed two days to get results. This friend called the University of Chicago Medical Center and got in touch with someone over the weekend. A nurse from there called us first thing Monday morning. We felt blessed. Meetings were falling into place – but for the long weekend, we waited.

Monday morning, we got a call at 9:00 am to set up the PET scan on Tuesday at 9:30 am. Now, there is a 24-hour fast necessary – God set up the perfect timing. This perfect timing was followed by a call from the University of Chicago Medical Center to see an oncologist on Wednesday. We questioned if the PET scan results could be ready by then since we were told to go to the doctor in Naperville on Thursday because they needed 48 hours to read the PET scan. They confirmed that we could bring the CD with us from the test on Tuesday.

We asked our friend Bill to go with us. Since he had survived prostate cancer a year earlier, he told us it was good to have an extra pair of ears available when you are hearing important medical information! As we sat in that office, it was difficult to pretend anything else was on our mind – anything but the reality that we were about to hear where cancer was detected in David's body. I think we all would have guessed that it had traveled, if we talked about it. Having the large amount outside his lung indicated it had already left its original site. But, those words weren't spoken. We hoped that somehow, we would hear good news from this doctor.

The doctor got to the point quickly.

"It has spread from its site of origin."

"Where?" David asked.

"Does it matter?" he answered.

I guess they are used to working with chemo packages that will attack it everywhere and I also think he didn't want to tell us.

So, surgery was not an option – removing the lung would not take away this problem.

He advised us of chemo options and his research program. The research program did have the possibility of using an experimental, new drug, but also came with the option of being given a placebo. We decided to see if the doctor in Naperville offered the same chemo. On Thursday, Dr. Lara did. Our office visit with her was wonderful. Hope was revealed.

She spoke of David's age being in his favor to fight this. He asked if he could hug her. We both felt the cloud lift in her office. The chemo package she offered was identical to the one we were offered downtown and much more convenient, so we signed up to begin chemo with her the following Monday. As a precaution, both doctors suggested a brain scan as one of the newer chemo drugs for lung cancer could cause bleeding and would not be an option if the cancer is in the brain. We scheduled the scan early Friday morning and were told they would have results by Monday, before beginning chemo. Dr. Lara called five hours after the scan.

I was downstairs, playing my Dr. Mario as an escape from my thoughts, when the phone rang. David called to me that Dr. Lara was on the phone. I ran upstairs. I got on the office phone as he sat in the living room and her words cut through both of us like a knife.

"It has shown up in three locations in the brain, so the chemo package is on hold. I will introduce you to a radiation oncologist to begin radiation of the brain immediately. We need to get the brain under control before beginning chemo."

As she continued to talk, Kevin walked in the room on his cell phone. He had been waiting all week for a call regarding a job offer and it came while we were on the phone with the doctor.

She continued to talk, recommending a radiation oncologist from Edward Hospital, Dr. McCall.

Kevin got the job he had worked so hard for at school, and David and I received news that David's brain had cancer cells. It was the absolute opposite extremes of emotion for all of us. How could we rejoice for Kevin's phone call while grasping the seriousness of David's phone call. I remember hugging Kevin, David did too, as we congratulated him and watched him try to receive our congratulations as his eyes welled up with tears for his dad.

Dr. McCall's office called us that afternoon. We were on an emotional roller coaster. They scheduled us to begin brain radiation on Monday and we braced ourselves for another long weekend of waiting.

David posted the following on Caring Bridge:

"Unfortunately, with the results of the brain scan, it appears that we can no longer use the effective, 'smart,' new drug that they were planning to use in my chemo because it has risks of exploding and bleeding as side effects which are unacceptable risks for the brain. So, after two weeks of radiation therapy, they will develop another chemo package. The good news is the doctors are still hopeful and do think the radiation and chemotherapy will be successful. The other Good News is that I was tapped on the shoulder to see if I would be willing to sit this game out and let a substitute take my place. At first, I was a bit taken aback because I like to be in charge. Hitting the final home run, dropping the last putt, and just kind of being in control. But, He asked me if I've ever won this battle before and He told me that

He already has – so Jesus is taking my place on the team and I'm going to rest on the bench along with the rest of my supporters and cheer."

We walked through that weekend in a fog as the severity of his diagnosis began to take root. David was really sick. Seriously sick. Talking with the radiation oncologist, we set up an appointment for Monday and she prescribed steroids in the meantime.

I ran to make it to the store for anything that would help David, and as I quickly exited our driveway, good friends, Dave and Sara, were walking past our home. I stopped long enough to say to them "This is shitty – this is so shitty!" They were surprised – I had usually chosen my words more carefully. When I got home and he took the steroids, he noticed improvement quickly. By Saturday morning, he felt like his old self again.

Monday morning, we arrived and met a wonderful woman, who immediately hugged us because we were friends of Bill's. She told us we were now family! David was measured for the mask used in brain radiation and we left for lunch, only to return later that day for the first treatment. I drove him on Tuesday, and he drove himself on Wednesday. It was a glorious day – we were doing what needed to be done to fight this cancer and David was feeling good. After his first week of brain radiation, there would be three more before we began chemo.

During that week, David received a great gift. Erin and Donny made up t-shirts with our family name on the front and a number on the back to depict a team coming together to fight this battle. We took pictures and prayed together. David was thrilled and so proud of his family.

One afternoon, he signaled for me to stay in the living room with

Erin and Macy. He said he needed time alone. He closed the door, laid on the floor and wept. We had the TV on in our room, but I could hear some of his sobs. I prayed and waited. He came out ten minutes later and told me he had heard from God. He said he could fight this battle now because he had surrendered it to God and God gave him assurance that he was not alone. He was greatly comforted and strengthened in spirit.

We had a somewhat quiet Saturday until the evening. He asked me to feel a lump in the lower calf of his left leg. He told me he didn't want to alarm me, but we had to consider the possibility of a blood clot. I asked him if we should go to the hospital to get it checked out and he said he would sleep on that decision. When I awoke at 7 o'clock on Sunday morning and entered his office, he said he thought we should have it checked out. So, we left for Good Samaritan Hospital. After several hours in the emergency room, it was determined to be a large clot – in fact, the admitting nurse who felt it simply said – "Oh my! That's fricken huge!" – we laughed with her because David often used the word fricken when he was upset and we hadn't heard it a lot otherwise. They ordered a chest X-ray and ultrasound and after admitting us to the hospital room around 7 o'clock that night, the nurse mentioned that the test was positive.

"Positive?" we asked.

"Yes," she said, "the clot has broken off and tiny bits are in your lung."

"Oh," we replied as she left the room.

So, when the staff had time, we sat down to discuss what that meant. Well, it was not good. David had to stay completely still – not even get up to use the bathroom, and the next 48 hours would be crucial for his body. We chose the intravenous blood thinner. At first, we wanted to go home with Coumadin and shots, but, since it had left the leg and entered the lung, we were both very glad we had decided to stay in the hospital on the stronger blood thinner. We both slept okay that night, but the second night in the hospital, he awoke in pain – chest pain – exactly what they didn't want to happen. I jumped up and pressed the nurse call button with one hand and tried raising the bed with the other – they immediately helped raise him up to a sitting position and he was relieved. The pain ceased and a bullet was dodged.

They told us we needed to wait for his blood level to get to a therapeutic level – until then, they drew blood every six hours – this took days and he felt like a pin cushion. Finally, on Wednesday, it was an acceptable level of "thinness" and we were given the okay to leave on Thursday with Coumadin and shots. The shots were to be given every 12 hours.

We left the hospital on Thursday and went straight to brain radiation, since we had missed some treatments. We were excited to be back in the fight and even asked Dr. McCall to consider radiating the lung. We had seen pictures from Dr. Yu in the hospital and it was really full of liquid. We hoped that radiating it would relieve some of the discomfort for David and get rid of some of the tumor/fluid buildup. She asked him if he was on any pain medicine and he said no. She gave him some Tylenol with codeine, just in case he wanted something at home. He did decide to take a little to help him sleep at night, because the Ambien was not giving him a good night's sleep. He couldn't seem to go into a deep sleep with it.

By Sunday afternoon, David was very uncomfortable. Dr. McCall called to see how he was doing, because she had seen him very weak on

Saturday, at the radiation appointment. Hope revealed itself through her call. She had used her husband's cell phone because her phone couldn't get a cell connection in that area. God in action through her – contacting us on a Sunday afternoon because God knew we needed her to tell us to go to the hospital.

"David is not eating much and is very constipated. I have gone to the drug store and purchased everything imaginable to help him, but no bowel movement. He is very uncomfortable."

"I think you should take him in," she said.

I was relieved and so was he several hours later. They found that his counts were high on magnesium, and gave him something to drink to release it from his body. He had a miserable night because he was in the bathroom continually, but once it cleared up, he felt much better.

David was fighting valiantly – as well as any warrior ever could – and we were released a few days later to continue with radiation treatments. We chose to stop the lung radiation treatments for now and just concentrate on finishing the brain treatments. His body was fighting, but we needed to help it and we were maybe a little aggressive. They kept assuring us that this was a slow growing cancer, but we really wanted to "zap" it as quickly as possible.

Once home, David had fun writing on the Caring Bridge web site – telling a Biblical story about a bald prophet – his sense of humor was amazing. He was in a very serious battle for his physical body and he was adding humor to the outlook. God, in him, was amazing.

THEREFORE WE DO NOT LOSE HEART. THOUGH OUTWARDLY WE ARE WASTING AWAY, YET INWARDLY WE ARE BEING RENEWED DAY BY DAY. — II CORINTHIANS 4:16

After a troubled evening, we saw three doctors on Thursday, April

24th in order to better understand how to help his body through this. We all agreed to begin weaning him off of the steroids, because as much as they helped in the beginning, they had now caused some problems for him physically. The blood thinner shots were trying – he wanted to do them himself, yet he was weak. So, he would insert the needle and I would push the serum in. When one of the areas of entrance continued to bleed, I changed his shirt five times before calling a nurse friend and finding out the correct way to stop the bleeding.

I think that when you are in the midst of helping someone you love go through a difficult time, you don't think straight. She didn't tell me anything I didn't know, but I couldn't comprehend how to focus on the project at hand. My life seemed like a play and I was an actress going along with the motions – kind of in a fog. Was this all really happening or would I wake up soon and find this all to be a bad, very bad dream?

We asked Bill to accompany us to a doctor visit on Monday morning, April 28th. David's strength was not coming back yet and I wanted help getting him in and out of the car. It was wonderful that Bill could accompany us because when the oncologist looked at his blood count numbers, she sent us to the hospital immediately. Bill drove us there and we set up for another stay to get his magnesium count back to a normal level. By Wednesday, he felt much better. Since he felt good, the doctor stopped in and asked his permission to begin chemo that day. David looked at me and listened to her. He agreed to begin chemo. I walked the hospital grounds listening to praise music for the first hour, because he had to be monitored carefully. He slept part of the afternoon and, when I left in the evening, he was watching the Cubs and feeling tired, but good.

Thursday morning, he called me as I drove back to the hospital and his voice indicated a different tone. He was extremely weak and each syllable took effort. When I arrived, we spoke a little and a nephew stopped in to say hi. The day progressed in slow motion – waiting for him to get energy that never arrived. In fact, around 1:00 PM, I called the doctor's office from outside his room to ask what was going on. I remember asking her nurse to mention to the doctor that my husband looked like he was on his last breath – what exactly was happening? The head oncology nurse, who was wonderful, stopped in to assure me that they just don't know with cancer. You can look like you are on your last breath and rally – or you can *be* on your last breath. David struggled all day. He couldn't move at all, so I called nurses to help with anything he needed. It was a quiet day as I waited for his body to rally and he tried to find energy to move.

Around 6:00 PM he said to me, "Hon, I don't want another day like this."

"Let's see what the doctor says, hon," I said.

And, in she walked – *Hope Revealed*. God sent an oncologist to his bedside at 6:00 PM when she had visited us in the morning.

"Why is he so weak?" I asked. "Is it from the chemo or the cancer?"

"David," she said, sitting on one side of the bed holding his hand as I sat on the other side holding his other hand, "It looks like the cancer has taken over your body."

Do not let your hearts be troubled. Trust in God; trust also in me. In my Father's house are many rooms; if it were not so, I would have told you. I am going there to prepare a place for you. And if I go and prepare a place for you, I will come back and take you to be with me that you also may be where I am. — John 14:1-3

"Well, then," he said matter-of-factly, "make me comfortable. The next time I open my eyes, I want to see Jesus."

⟶ ☙ ⟵

THE LORD DELIGHTS IN THOSE WHO FEAR HIM, WHO PUT THEIR HOPE IN HIS UNFAILING LOVE. — PSALM 147:11

FOURTEEN

Ready To Go To Heaven

He knew his Savior – he knew God's Word and what promises would be revealed when he gave over his spirit.

The doctor looked at him and asked if he wanted to go home to Aurora. She said she could send all the bells and whistles to his bedside at home.

"I've already let go of that home," he said. "I'm ready for my new home and my new body."

She looked at me.

As I met her eyes, I said, "He is uncomfortable if he is moved at all. I don't want him moved."

"That is the nicest thing you have ever said to me," David said.

And that was it – the beginning of the end of his fight. The doctor instructed the nurses to stop all medications except one intravenous tube left in for pain meds. He had an oxygen tube in his nose left in for his comfort.

David lay back and closed his eyes. I left the room and called the children. Dad was going home and they could come by to say they loved him, but his body had given out and he was ready to see Jesus. Each child in the area arrived within an hour and spoke words of love to him through tears. We stood together for a short time as he said "you're all going to have wonderful lives." We responded quietly, "because of you." He closed his eyes with a smile. By midnight, Erika and her fiance arrived from Michigan and I gave them the same instructions.

"He is ready to go to heaven. Give him your blessing to go."

By God's grace, we were all able to let go of the man that God used to make us a family, the man who loved us and taught us how to love others, the man who gave each of us an example of living God's way, the man who picked up our pieces, encouraged us through tough times, gave of himself continually and never asked for anything for himself. Now, he was asking to go to heaven and we wanted, more than anything else, for him to be comfortable. So, we let him go.

By 1:30 AM, David and I bunkered down for our last night together. He was trying to relax and sleep in the hospital bed and I tried to get comfortable in the chair next to it. I would hear "Hon?" often because his throat was drying out, so I would get up and bring the straw of a glass of water up to his lips. He said the water tasted like heaven to his throat. I wiped his head often and changed his pillowcase because he seemed to be sweating profusely, like sweating out a fever. Someone walked in with a machine twice – we both sat up quickly.

"NO MORE!"

We didn't know what they wanted to measure, but no more measuring, poking, prodding – no more. He was being released from his body and we didn't allow any more needles to touch it – any medical readings meant nothing to us. The morning came quickly.

It took me until morning to realize that the dryness was worse for him because of the oxygen. Since he wasn't having any discomfort breathing, I took off the oxygen tube.

He didn't ask for any more water.

A grimace here and there, and a desire to stay in a relaxed position. David began to get ready by denying much communication. He spoke very little. He lay there calmly, handling the day one moment at a time. Once the doctor said the cancer had taken over his body, he prepared to leave it. He turned his life over to God and took away the medical staff's ability to try to keep his body alive. He began to relax and accept his journey to heaven.

FOR TO ME, TO LIVE AS CHRIST AND TO DIE IS GAIN. — PHILIPPIANS 1:21

The children came back early and we took shifts going to the cafeteria. Why try to eat? Habit? There was no other reason. I had no desire for food or anything – well, maybe one desire – that this was all a bad dream and we would wake up soon.

Some phone calls began coming in because most people didn't know how quickly it had turned so serious. One sister-in-law called and asked if her two sons could come over. We left the room for David to have a few words with them.

Even though his voice was strained, they clearly understood his first words.

"What day is it?"

"Friday."

"Then, why aren't you two at work?"

Uncle Dave was always a joker.

By 10:30 AM, our daughters sat at his bedside reading Scripture out loud. The rest of us went in and out and finally, I decided to stay in with them. I noticed his breathing seemed to be slowing down so I called all the children. We stood around his bed as the Scriptures were being read and we all joined hands. David was in a big circle of love, even though I'm not sure he was even aware of us. And, then, as his chest started rising less, we began singing *How Great Thou Art*.

We don't have gifted voices, but it was a sweet sound. David's mouth moved, for the first time in an hour or so, twice during the refrain. I have no doubt he was singing with us. Then, his chest rose for the last time and as it quieted and lay still, our singing became sobbing. I believe Jesus

How Great Thou Art

Oh Lord, my God, when I in awesome wonder
Consider all the worlds Thy hands have made
I see the stars, I hear the rolling thunder
Thy power throughout the universe displayed

When Christ shall come with shouts of acclamation
And take me home, what joy shall fill my heart!
Then I shall bow in humble adoration,
And there proclaim, my God, how great Thou art!

Then sings my soul
My Savior God to Thee
How great Thou art
How great Thou art [3]

took him right from the bed at Good Samaritan Hospital up to hear the angels sing. I believe he went from our voices to theirs – and it must have been marvelous for him.

I walked over to sit next to him, as his face had turned to the right and as I sat down, I closed his eyes. I pulled the sheet up to his chin and waited. I remember asking for a friend, JoAnn, to come pray with me. I knew some friends were downstairs in the chapel praying during the morning. God surrounded us with love through His servants. JoAnn prayed over me for a while and time stood still. I do remember someone coming in – I think a chaplain – to pronounce his body dead – but I knew he was still alive – he had just given up his flesh.

Thinking back, as I watched his body, all day long, getting weaker and weaker; as I watched him struggle just to sit up and then give up on sitting up; as I noticed his face grimace as the pain started to get in touch with his feelings – I saw a resemblance of giving birth.

As I focused on the medicine dripping slowly into his vein, I saw a birthing process. The body relaxes under the pain medicine and slowly slumbers into a dreamy state. As his breathing became shallow, and the birthing drew nearer, he opened his eyes less and less. He remained extremely calm in anticipation of his future – he knew where he was going. His body accepted and tolerated the medication. He slowly released his spirit.

FATHER, INTO YOUR HANDS I COMMIT MY SPIRIT. — LUKE 23:46

Turning his head to the side to sing along with us, his mouth moved in unison to our song while a peace enveloped him. His breathing became slower and then there was a pause between breaths. Slowly, he took his final breath and his chest lay still under the light veiling of a hospital gown. His eyes were open as his spirit rose from his body and joined Jesus in the company of angels. As I sat next to him and waited – waited to be sure this was happening – I realized I had witnessed his birthing into new life – God's gift of eternal life. Knowing how much he loved exploring, I smiled slightly at the thought of his new adventure. Then, the reality of my new adventure began to surface – David no longer walking beside me on this earth.

My reality.

I called Bob at the funeral home of David's choice.

"If the Lord takes me home, Hon, do you know where I want to have the wake and do you know where the cemetery plot is?"

"Yes, honey, I know."

Bob said he would be over in a little while to pick him up. He wanted us to take as much time as we needed with him. But, I thought, David isn't here anymore – why would we stay here?

I started to gather things in the room and when I opened the closet to pack some things, I couldn't get passed seeing his brown jacket. He wore that jacket so often and I loved how it felt. I would snuggle up to it in the car – hold it with my arm under his and lean against it for his support. I slumped to my knees and started emitting sounds I hadn't heard before – I believe it's called wailing. My daughter brought me a chair and I sobbed and I sobbed. My head got dizzy and I realized my daughter was sitting in front of me telling me to breathe. I think I was, but I wasn't conscious of anything much other than David didn't need this jacket anymore.

I stumbled around that room. His shoes – those gym shoes he used so many times to take walks – wow – this tremendous pain. This was emotional pain at a new level for me. The kids asked me to take his things home and decide later what to do with them. I listened.

When I arrived home, friends had dropped off food. The children were hungry and grateful. I was so grateful, but not aware if I was hungry. I talked to Bob about meeting on Saturday to set up arrangements and posted on the Caring Bridge web site that David went home to heaven. A fog took over my brain – a deep, dense fog encompassed my thinking and emotions. After posting on the web-site, I began to write. I knew I needed to talk at the funeral.

All the children went with me to the funeral home to make arrangements the next day.

"This is good, right?" I said to Bob, after picking out everything necessary.

"No, this is not good. David shouldn't have gone to heaven yet."

"I mean, we did good with what we picked out, didn't we?"

"Yes."

As I began to leave the funeral parlor for my car, I remembered David's wedding ring. There it was, in a pocket in my purse. His fingers had become swollen and I took it off so it wouldn't hurt to get it off later. I told him we would put it back on when the swelling went down. The next day, he was more swollen and he said, "Good call on the ring, honey!" I asked Bob if the swelling went down after he went to heaven and he said his fingers were still swollen. So I asked if they could place his right hand over his left hand, in the casket, so no one would notice a ring missing. Bob said they could. Then I approached David's daughter and her fiance. They were to be married later that month. I produced dad's ring, gently rubbing it back and forth in my hand.

"Would you like to get this sized and wear dad's wedding ring for your marriage to his daughter," I asked.

"I would be honored," he said.

All three of us cried. David was a recycler, a garbage man. I know he would like the ring being recycled to represent another union.

On Sunday, friends and a pastor came over to discuss the service. We put the timing of songs and talks together rather quickly. I told them I would like to speak and practiced it at the table. I don't know if they were just being kind, but they told me not to change it and I tried not to look at it again until Tuesday morning. I was blessed to have two pastors at the service. They were Christ with flesh on for me and blessed the funeral service tremendously. The wake was only one night, Monday, and it was a long night. So many wonderful lives that David touched – through his life and the lives of his children. So many wonderful stories of how he blessed someone in business. He had used

God's gifts of administration and business excellently in his life here on earth.

NOW TO HIM WHO IS ABLE TO DO IMMEASURABLY MORE THAN ALL WE ASK OR IMAGINE, ACCORDING TO HIS POWER THAT IS AT WORK WITHIN US. — EPHESIANS 3:20

When I arrived home from the wake, there was a call from Colorado. The "home" David's son lived in wanted me to talk to him about David. The last time either of us spoke to him, he was not living in reality and I wanted to wait a month or so to fly to Denver and tell him in person. They wanted it sooner. I mentioned this to the children and David's daughter mentioned it to her Uncle Jim. He graciously flew to Denver the following weekend to tell him of the loss of David to his life. His son cried and seemed to understand. I called when they were together and we had a nice conversation. I was so grateful I didn't have to get on a plane yet.

Some friends had asked to pray over me before the service on Tuesday morning, so when I arrived, we gathered downstairs in the church. It was a wonderful time of prayer and as we ended, some old friends from the village hall arrived, and I introduced them around. Jim, a police officer who knew both of us, came to lead the procession. I was so honored for David to have a police escort.

→ ψ ←

WE WHO HAVE FLED TO TAKE HOLD OF THE HOPE OFFERED TO US MAY BE GREATLY ENCOURAGED. WE HAVE THIS HOPE AS AN ANCHOR FOR THE SOUL, FIRM AND SECURE. — HEBREWS 6:18B-19

FIFTEEN

Like Part of Me Had Been Cut Off

As I looked at David in the casket before the service began, I studied his face. I had studied his face many times over the years while giving him a face trace. He would lie down on the couch, with his head on my lap and close his eyes while the TV played in the background. I would gently trace his features around and around until he fell asleep. He would snore and I would lift his head off my lap and onto a pillow. Then, when I was ready to go to bed, I would gently awake him and walk him to bed. He stayed half asleep during the walk and it was so wonderful to see him so relaxed.

Next, I studied his eyebrows because I had trimmed them – time and time again. I began giving David haircuts when we dated and he hadn't had a professional one since. I was such an amateur, but he always said that he didn't have enough hair to pay to have it clipped. His Dutch heritage taught him to be frugal. I had a nose trimmer, electric razor for the top bald part and clippers for the sides. I used a comb and scissors on his eyebrows as he didn't like tweezing.

He wasn't particular but liked it kept short, so we spent a lot of time together over the sink. I miss taking care of his hair – it was one of the few ways I was able to care for such an independent man.

As we walked in behind the casket, they played his favorite worship version of *Holy, Holy, Holy* and, as the song escalated, I knew my arm and hand were moving upward, next to my head. My arm was reaching in worship for my Savior as I prepared to attend my husband's funeral. I'm so grateful I didn't have to think about it; my body just responded.

David had asked, while in the hospital, that four gentlemen speak at his funeral. They each accepted, even one that David changed his mind about because he thought he was too busy. I asked David to let the individual make that decision. David emphasized that they not talk about him, but about what God did through him.

The talks couldn't have been sweeter. Each one pointing out a part of his life, from his family to his business to his ministry, and how God had used his servant, David, to bless others' lives.

Rob:

When Mary called to invite me to say a few words today, she shared a little anecdote that gave me a further appreciation for how considerate Dave was. Two weeks ago, when they were discussing a list of people who might say something at his funeral, Dave thought my name should be on that list.

A day or two later, however, he told Mary, "Let's take Rob off that list, he's too busy," knowing that I have a pretty full plate right now at work and in the construction of our new church. That was just like Dave, always considerate of the other person. Mary counseled him to leave it up to me to determine if I was too busy; I'm up here today because I'm not.

I'm quite certain that Dave knew what I would talk about on this occasion because, over the years, we often marveled together at the way God used a golf weekend in French Lick, Indiana, to initiate His purpose in my life. Proverbs 19:21 is a verse that speaks to our plans and God's purpose. It has given me an understanding and perspective on what really happened when we went on that golf outing twenty-five years ago.

MANY ARE THE PLANS IN A MAN'S HEART, BUT IT IS THE LORD'S PURPOSE THAT PREVAILS. – PROVERBS 19:21

For the initial nine years of my engineering career, the first half of Proverbs 19:21 was in full force. I had plans to be a very good civil engineer working in a large firm on interesting projects throughout this country and around the world. In 1983, the Lord redirected those plans into a path that was consistent with His Purpose for my life; that Purpose was to use the talents He had entrusted to me to begin and build a consulting engineering firm.

God used a number of circumstances and a variety of people to redirect my plans; but none more significant than the involvement of two brothers who owned HDS – Harvey Bulthuis and David Bulthuis. When I shared with Dave on that infamous golf trip my dream of starting my own civil engineering firm, Dave asked if I had considered using venture capital to assist with the start-up. Displaying my ignorance, I asked him what venture capital was. Dave quickly recognized that it was not going to be a simple project to take a civil engineer and turn him into a business entrepreneur – but he and Harv graciously persisted.

With the benefit of their wisdom, insights, and encouragement, I was able to launch a fledgling consulting firm and over the last 25 years, it has grown into a respected and reputable firm.

I share that with you not so much as a direct tribute to either Harv or Dave, and certainly not to me, but rather as a testimony to the sovereignty and supremacy of God's purpose in our lives. His purpose for my life was, and is, the business that I now lead.

He used two wonderful friends and mentors, Harv for a few years, and Dave for a much longer period of time, to guide and encourage me in my ministry.

I am so grateful to have known Dave as a brother in Christ, a good friend and one of the people that a sovereign God used to direct His purposes in my life. I'm thankful too that one of the many facets of Dave's legacy is a consulting engineering firm that has been built on the Biblical principles that Dave himself modeled in both his business and his life. Indeed, he has been a most effective instrument in the Lord's prevailing Purpose in the lives of family, friends and business partners. To God Be the Glory!

Matt:

I feel a little inadequate speaking here today. I never golfed with my Uncle Dave, but many here would say that to golf with him is to know him. I do know that golf was one of his great passions.

I worked for Uncle Dave some summers at HDS, but I never worked nearly as close as many of the people here.

I did not go to his church and didn't get to see him often in the last few years.

But he was my Uncle. And only a few here have known him as an Uncle. So I wanted to share a little about that and help you to know him from my perspective.

My earliest memories of my Uncle Dave were from holidays at my Grandpa and Grandma's house on Wolf Road. He was always quick with a smile and a joke. He always brought humor and cheer to every function and we looked forward to seeing him for that reason. He was athletic. Summers at Gun Lake we could always expect a performance on the skis from Uncle Dave. I remember a time that he was hot dogging with the slalom ski and took a bad spill, literally burying his head in the muck at the bottom of the lake. I remember being very worried, but he was *alright. He was always alright. Later on Uncle Dave had a great house for family gatherings, with a big backyard for football and Frisbee, and better yet, a basement with a pool table, where all of us cousins could gather and reconnect, hang out and play pool. I think that was a testament to his patience and generosity. Being a pool table owner now, I know how difficult it must have been for him to let a half dozen kids loose with pool cues in his basement. He always did. But the main thing I remember from those days of being a kid and the family gatherings was his good humor. I pitied any boyfriend that came to a Bulthuis holiday, because I knew they were going to get the ribbing from Uncle Dave that the rest of us so looked forward to. I still feel that Uncle Dave was an example of the kind of uncle that I strive to be. And I thank him for that example.*

He was a fair and firm boss at HDS. All of us family members coming into the business must have been tough, but in my experience he never coddled us and always treated us fairly. There may have been a few incidents where some of us may have received a little extra leniency, but I don't think we want to get into that now. Let's just say he was firm, but patient.

After I left HDS, I knew Uncle Dave as a generous man. Anything he had he was willing to share with his nieces and nephews. He generously offered his place in Wisconsin to my wife Cathy and I and we spent a wonderful weekend there. He had an open invitation for us to use his condo in Florida. I think his generosity was a good example for me as well.

As I became an adult and had a family of my own, he treated me with respect, as an equal, as an adult. Which I can imagine would be hard for an uncle to a nephew. It's hard to describe exactly the feeling, but I guess its like a graduation from childhood. Its a good feeling. He called me whenever he had computer problems, and he trusted my judgment and recommendations. And whenever I was out to his house to fix a computer or help with something, the first thing I received was a huge smile, a warm handshake, and a pat on the back. Even if I hadn't seen him for months or a year, there was never any doubt that he was glad to see me and was genuinely concerned and caring about myself and my family. Any computer problems were always less important than that.

So five weeks ago when I heard that he was diagnosed with cancer, I went to his Caring Bridge website and left a message of support for him. This started a time of sharing, via e-mails, with my Uncle Dave that I will always hold very dear in my heart. Getting to know him better in the last few weeks has deepened my love for him as well as my regret for not spending more time with him in the last 10 years. He knew that I liked music and playing guitar, and told me about his days in high school and college when he sang with a group that actually performed some shows including a battle of the bands in LaGrange. He told me about his college days when he started doing comedy skits and found out that he was not cut out for teaching, which was his major. He told me about HDS, starting there as, as he put it, "the owner's youngest college dropout son." He told me about the early difficulties and ultimate blessings of working with his brother, my Uncle Harvey. And he told me how blessed he was that God surrounded him with people more gifted than him in mechanics, sales, operations, and administration. And he told me how now, after HDS, he is growing and thriving, desiring to be God's vehicle.

Throughout this time of sharing he was undergoing treatments and getting weaker, having ups and downs, and suffering. But he kept that positive attitude and good humor. He and Mary also used this time to be a witness for the Lord. Setting an example for Christians to find hope and contentment in the Lord even in times of difficulty, and showing a peace that anyone who was not a Christian surely would not understand, and hopefully would want to know more about.

Last Thursday Mary called me and gave me the opportunity to come by and see Uncle Dave. We had missed an opportunity the week before. I figured I would stop by in the afternoon on the way to an appointment. Around noon I left to get lunch at my favorite deli, a place that I usually go to at least twice a week, right up the street from my office. As I was driving there, I really felt that instead of eating a sandwich, I should probably go to the hospital. I kept driving anyway and was shocked when I got there and saw that the deli was closed. Out of business. I said, OK Lord. I'm sorry. I am going to Good Sam right now. I called Aunt Mary and she said it was a good time to come and so I did. I am so thankful that I went. When I walked into the room, despite his weakness and discomfort, he had a huge smile on his face. He took my hand a we talked a little about work and family. He told me I work too much and that going gray was better than going bald. When I told him I was short on staff at my office, he started trying to think of a good employee for me.

When I sensed it was time to go and Uncle Dave's eyes were closed, I got up and he surprised me by gripping my hand again. I turned, and he said two words to me that he had never said to me before. He said "Love You." And I think that maybe that was the message he wanted everyone here to get. To all the nieces and nephews, friends and other relatives that may not have gotten the chance to see him one last time. That was the message that he would have given to you. Whether he said it in life or not, he loved you.

Chris:

When I was asked to say a few words here today about David Bulthuis, I thought, "Where do I start?" It is an honor and blessing to have shared in his life and to be up here right now sharing some of my experiences with Dave.

I'm going to start with the big picture first.

He gets to spend eternity with thousands of people coming to him and saying "You had a part in me being here."

Dave wore many hats with me: my ministry partner, my boss, a founder of Lampstand Ministries, a friend, a Father figure

– and – I don't know about you, but I'm experiencing Dave Bulthuis withdrawal right now – nobody can replace Dave.

Out of the 13 years of working with Dave, he has never raised his voice at me except when he was excited about something. I would come to him with many ideas and if I talked to my wife Naomi and the idea was "real brilliant," she would say, "I'll agree to that if you go and run it past Dave real quick." And, when it was a "brilliant" idea and we would be sitting there having breakfast – he would always order his eggs "with a little cheese melted on top" – and I would give him my idea and if the idea was questionable, he would do this with his mouth (making faces) and say, "Chris, I'm going to tell you this – you might not like it, but I have four reasons why I don't think it is a good idea." And, he would do this with a smile on his face.

BUT, if he liked something, he would get very red in the face and say "very good, young man, very good." When Dave was on board with something, as many of you know, he was 100% behind you. If he was going to go out to breakfast with you and discuss something, he would give you his all. He always made time for his friends. I would call him up and he would say, "Chris, I'm about to putt, but let me know what's going on."

He always answered his phone. He was always there for me.

And, out of the three things I think God showed me through Dave – because many times God uses people to express Himself to us – the three things I can think of are tenderness – because he was always tender – even if they were bad ideas – always tender.

He was always merciful. I remember calling him up and saying "Dave, I made a mistake. I'm so dumb." He would say "Chris, you are too hard on yourself. You know what – God's not worried about it, so I'm not worried about it. He's got our back covered."

And that's just the way Dave was.

He showed God's faithfulness. I remember when I first met him, I referred to him as Mr. Bulthuis and as our relationship culminated – you know when you start something together you get to learn a lot about each other – and right now, I would easily call him my pal Dave, my partner Dave, my buddy Dave.

And, even though I would make mistakes and both of us would make mistakes, he still hung in there. I'm thinking when is this guy going to leave and say, "this guy is hopeless" – but he never left. He was there from the beginning and he was my partner and my friend to the very end. I'm looking forward to the day when I can see him again in heaven. I think, if there are two things he would want to tell all of us right now, it would be that he loves us and "Do you know Jesus Christ?" because right now he is looking at the face of Almighty God and sitting at the feet of Jesus.

Cal:

Dave always liked to give me hard assignments. As a brother-in-law, he would give me toys that I couldn't put together for my kids or he would give me toys that were so loud I couldn't think. Dave would always do things that would push me.

But, I'm going to try to do this today. I'm going to try to give you a quick summary of Dave's life.

I knew him well, but, not until he married Charlene. That was about 38 years ago. I knew him before that, but from a distance. Some of you knew him well before he married Charlene and, without insider knowledge you have of that time, I'm going to go out on a limb and tell you that Dave, for a time, believe it or not, was a cocky, self-absorbed teenager who was pretty much fun and wasn't too worried about anything but fun. He was a hot shot junior when I was a tender freshman. Do you know a guy like that? It doesn't matter, because it all changed.

In 1973, Dave and Char came over to our house and told us they had really big news. Before that time, Dave and Char had a different world view than Marcy and I did. That day, the news was, they were born again. Nothing was the same after that. Dave and Char became transformed people and worked very hard at being leaders in this church and care givers to the hurting. For a time, life was very good for Dave and Char.

But, then, life became full of tragedies for David. Charlene became very ill and died. Dave took a lot of hits. I was with him during those times, as were many of you, and saw him cry out to God for strength and wisdom when nothing made sense.

I saw him grow in adversity.

A couple of years after Charlene died, David married Mary and I got to see him re-energized for life and take on a whole other world of opportunities.

When Dave and Mary got together, a team was formed. A team was formed that saw worlds converge and they were able to take on life together in ways they never could have alone. I saw Dave grow exponentially into a servant leader. Mary was so good for Dave and Dave was so good for Mary.

Throughout his life, Dave always had a great sense of humor. He was always full of fun and he had a grin on his face and a sparkle in his eyes. Dave was my dear friend and my "go to" guy. He was a man I completely confided in and trusted. He had the unusual ability to understand people. He was the "go to" guy for my wife and kids, too. His wisdom was based on reality. And, he would listen to your issues, give them great consideration and then follow up.

Dave didn't like to leave things hanging. He always dotted his "I's" and crossed his "T's." He was fun loving and caring, compassionate and encouraging. He understood what it took to build relationship and he always hoped for the best in others.

Last Thursday night, when I last visited Dave, I saw a Godly man totally at peace with his Father's will. He, who started out as a typically self-absorbed child, ended his life fully surrendered *to his Father's will. His love for family and friends became his greatest joy.*

He served God by being a loving husband to Mary, a loving Father to his children and grandchildren and to all of us who were blessed by touching life with him. He had become a servant leader who cared far more about others than himself and he died well, knowing perfect peace.

Dave learned to take adversity and let God shape him through it. He never became bitter, he just became better.

He finished the race and finished strong. I will always thank God for my brother and friend, David Bulthuis.

What a gift he was.

We, as his family, were so proud to have been chosen by God to walk alongside David. So proud.

He had been in the military, yet I couldn't find discharge papers. As God intervened, they were still able to get gentlemen to play taps at the grave site and hand me a flag. David used to enjoy being in church on Memorial Day weekend when they asked anyone who had served to stand up. It wasn't the applause he enjoyed as much as the recognition for the time he devoted to serving this country. So, I knew it would mean a lot to have the military acknowledge his service at his grave site and am so grateful that Bob at the funeral home was able to work it out. So grateful.

Leaving him at the grave site was difficult. It felt so *separate.* Like we were separated. Like part of me was staying here and the other part had to keep moving. Being pulled away. I use the term amputation – not lightly. But, it was like part of me had been cut off and if I left the grave site, I was not able to get it back.

Time passes very slowly sometimes and returning home was

painful. Walking around the home, I would wait to hear him call my name or shout "Hon." He would call it from room to room and I could hear it in every room. Looking for him in the bedroom, bathroom, downstairs, garage – not intentionally, just habitually – and needing to keep remembering "Oh yeah, David is in heaven." I must have said it a thousand times a day that first week.

We ate every meal together, so the kitchen was way too painful and I wasn't at all interested in going to the grocery store. He would be in the next aisle, usually the soup aisle, finding himself a treat or two and catch up with the cart. He always looked at my list and ran for things. I liked to take my time, but he was on a hunt and always put things in the cart and darted for another "find." It took me about three months to go down the soup aisle without crying. In fact, for the first few months, I picked up things through drive thru's or ate cereal. The thought of preparing food and setting out one plate was terrifying. I made myself do it one night – actually cooked meatloaf and mashed potatoes and green beans, set one place and as I sat looking out the window eating dinner, the pain was so intense and the tears so huge that I haven't done it again. I usually stand at the counter or make something small and sit watching TV with a tray. Someday I'll finish walking through that pain.

I started to work on thankfulness. I had learned this lesson many years ago, and pulled it out again. I discovered that when I said thank you, I couldn't stay downcast. Gratefulness and complaining just don't go together. So, anytime the tears began to flow I would say, thank you, God, and think of something about David in my life to be grateful for – which was easy. Just the fact that he chose to marry me is still amazing to me – God was directing that all the way. There were other women after him and God is the only reason he continued to pursue me.

I miss him.

I miss hearing his voice and talking to him. I talked so much – processed out loud so much – his poor ears got so tired and we laughed about it.

"Does every thought that enters your mind need to come out your mouth?" he asked once.

"Yes, I think it probably does." I said.

And we laughed.

"Honey, my ears hurt," he said once on a golf course.

And we laughed.

I miss him.

I miss his belly laughs – when tears would come to his eyes after he couldn't stop laughing. I miss hearing his laugh – hearing his joy in us. He took great joy in our relationship and brought me great joy. He understood me and accepted me exactly as I was – oh, yes, he would give suggestions on things I may want to change, but he accepted me as a work in progress and was patient with my growth. He loved me always – even when I snapped at him and would apologize. I was always forgiven and even though there were times he seemed irritated, he would quickly get over it and give me a hug. His hugs made everything in this world OK. No matter how difficult things seemed, when David hugged me, everything was going to be alright. He can't hug me now to give me that comfort, that reassurance that everything will be okay. I must receive it from God.

I'm not sure which is more difficult when you can't be with someone you love. Is it more difficult to be aware of their presence? Or to keep busy and when the calmness appears, remember – oh yeah – he is in heaven isn't he? Is it easier for the pain to be constant – constantly missing him? Or to go on each day trying not to focus on your loss and just be reminded with a fresh *pang*?

Meals – meals – we were together for so many meals. I was really hard on myself when they didn't turn out – but he wasn't. The look on his face when things weren't all together at the same time was priceless. We went through some difficult times with meals, but had it down pat toward the end. We ate so many meals together that we could have ordered for each other. He loved to take a bite of whatever I ordered. I think it looked better to him on someone else's plate, because he liked to taste food on the children's plates too. He loved little tastes of different foods. He would never eat the same food for two consecutive nights. At a restaurant, he would ask me what I was cooking the next night at home before ordering just to be sure it would be different. His favorite meal was little appetizers – a lot of them. One of our friend's annual Christmas party always featured unique appetizers and he loved that evening.

He also loved to sing at her parties. He would sing loudly, especially on a silly song about "bring me flesh and bring me something else." Oh, I love to remember him singing. His voice was sweet music to my ears.

I miss him.

I miss his joy and how much fun he made each day. Like going through the checkout line at the grocery.

"Do you need help outside?" they would ask.

"No, I have her," he would always answer.

Always – and I was so glad he had me, even though he wouldn't let me lift the groceries if he was around.

I miss him. I always will.

For the rest of my life on earth I will miss him and his joy – his winks, his jokes, his unconditional love. He truly showed me how to love unconditionally.

David and I talked often about love banks. I think we learned about them in a study by Gary Smalley and John Trent. Our hearts were like banks and we were able to make deposits and withdrawals. If I did something that hurt him, he would say, "It is a good thing you have enough deposits to cover that withdrawal!" I realized that David going to heaven is not a withdrawal. All the love he poured into me for the past years – all the deposits he made are still overflowing – my heart has lost nothing. Even though his physical presence is a good reinforcement, his love will always be a part of me and overflowing in my heart.

Macy was sleeping over at the house and I heard her groan a little in her sleep. I asked the Lord to bless her sleep and realized that her groan reminded me of my heart – always kind of whimpering – something amiss in my life – something off kilter – a little tilted – not quite straight.

I'm beginning to think that God and David are still enjoying what David contributed to this earth during his life here – watching the ripple effect. I thank God for David's life every day. I am so grateful that as David became weak – which I know was difficult for him – that he had peace from God that was amazing. David was totally comfortable with God's plan in his life.

I realized that I, during the first several months after he went to heaven, spent a lot of time reliving those weeks with the diagnosis.

My church offered a series called *One Month To Live* and I eagerly asked to speak about a wonderful man and how he handled his diagnosis and having one month to live. I spoke at two services and it was healing for me.

If anyone has a microphone and will listen to me talk about David, I'm there!

In fact, I was interviewed when the church wanted me to speak on the Beatitudes.

BLESSED ARE THOSE WHO MOURN, FOR THEY SHALL BE COMFORTED. — MATTHEW 5:4

I am living proof that God comforts us as we mourn.

During the taping of this interview, I told part of my story and mentioned how God helped me focus on how He answers our tough questions.

In God's goodness, He gives Scripture verses. Like when He answered Job.

WHO IS THIS THAT DARKENS MY COUNSEL WITH WORDS WITHOUT KNOWLEDGE? — JOB 38:2

I slowly raise my hand. Me, Lord.

I don't understand, Lord – You are God and I am not. And, I actually don't like what my life looks like without David in it – I really liked my life with David. But, because I know You love me and You love David, I am going to believe. Because of how big You are I can't even imagine Your plan, but it is going to be good.

WE ARE SORROWFUL YET REJOICING. — 2 CORINTHIANS 6:10

I am going to miss David every day for the rest of my life. By the grace of God, I am going to find joy every day for the rest of my life. Hope Revealed!

—❧ ✤ ❧—

NOW FAITH IS BEING SURE OF WHAT WE HOPE FOR AND CERTAIN FOR WHAT WE DO NOT SEE. — HEBREWS 11:1

SIXTEEN

Everything Was Different

In November, I had a dinner at the club to remember David. I invited those who golfed with him here these past years as well as the doctors who took care of him. Many accepted my invitation and I had fun preparing pictures for the tables. Each table had a name of something David liked and pictures to go along with it. One table was named "Water Sports," one "Teaching/Preaching" and so on. I had a short video made of pictures of him that used the song *Cherish* as background music. It was an anointed evening of celebration of a life well lived in service to God. It was also closure for me at the club and I was able to go there after that evening without crying.

I received a wonderful note

Cherish

Let's take a walk together near the ocean shore
Hand in hand you and I
Let's cherish every moment we have been given
The time is passing by
I often pray before I lay down by your side
If you receive your calling before I awake
Could I make it through the night
Cherish the love we have
We should cherish the life we live
Cherish the love, cherish the life, cherish the love
Cherish the love we have
For as long as we both shall live
Cherish the love, cherish the life, cherish the love [4]

from one of his doctors who couldn't attend the evening.

Dear Mary –

I am sorry that I was not able to be with you for David's Remembrance Dinner. I am thinking of you and your family over the holidays. Your beautiful witness of faith has prompted me to join a Bible study. I am grateful to you for "redirecting" me toward the Word.

Fondly, Anne McCall

By December, I realized that grieving was different for everyone. There is no right or wrong way to grieve. I read many books about it, but they sometimes had me focus on the loss instead of the healing I felt I wanted.

One thing I learned was that I had to keep my focus on how big God is, because otherwise, it became painful that He didn't have a different plan for David and I. How ungrateful that sounds as I write it. To think that I would question how long God gave me a gift – HA! What audacity! God gave me a great gift of a loving husband – a true blessing to my life – and I entertain thoughts of why He would take David to heaven before I was ready to let him go?

Also in December, I took a walk and as I passed the 17th hole of the golf course, covered in snow, I watched the soft blanket of white curve over the mounds as if it were alive, gently caressing the earth underneath. Then I saw under the blanket. The green grass of summer appeared and the many times David and I walked up to that tee box. No thoughts in our heads except this silly sport. And, then, like an old pain, it came – a reminder – I would never golf on that tee box with David again and never see him dance right after his tee shot if he liked it. This hole he rarely liked – the sand had become his friend and a constant companion as he tried to approach the green. But, I focused on his dance. He would have his club in hand and sway from side to side as he walked toward the cart, smiling boyishly.

When grieving chews on my emotions, my nerves aren't sure which way to go. Should I release the tension building up in me by letting the streams of tears flow? Or, is it time to replace the tension with reality and acceptance, thus minimizing the amount of time I will spend crying? Life will still be good – different but good. David would not like it if I spent too much time on how important he was to my emotional state. He would like it if I would enjoy life and remember him with love, not a biting pain chewing my emotions raw.

Getting ready for Christmas was unusual. Friends would speak of the difficulty of the *firsts* after a huge loss – *first* Christmas without him, *first* anniversary without him, *first* birthday without him. I think a lot of this pain is connected to routines or traditions. Occasions bring traditions and traditions often bring out roles. When a leading man is missing, and there is no understudy, the performance is clumsy.

Some traditions remain, but many need to be changed. David loved to shop and was good at it. Christmas shopping became painful, so I decided not to shop much. My focus was all over and I rarely knew what I had or had not accomplished. Decorating was not fun alone – I enjoyed his opinion on where the lights should go. Fortunately, my adult children are mature and all understood if their gifts or the time we spent together was a little askew. It was understood that mom was trying, but everything was different.

Unusual – that is the word.

Life seemed usual, prior to David's illness. I felt like I knew most of what to expect on any given day or week. Oh, there were surprises, of course, but my ship, glued to his, stayed on course. Throughout these months since he went to heaven, I have no idea if I am even on the ship, let alone on course. It is an unusual feeling. I've always told others that control is an illusion. I never realized how many things, each year, I did control with traditions and routines without even thinking about them until now – when I think of them because David isn't here for his role.

After Christmas and New Year's Eve, which is a wonderful time to spend with your grandchildren so your children can go out, something big hit me. When David lost his business, it took him six months to look seriously at me during dinner and say, "I hate getting up in the morning and having no where to go." I was thrilled because now we knew what the problem was, so we could begin a new routine for him and give him somewhere to go.

When David went to heaven, I not only lost my best friend, my lover, my traveling companion and my favorite meal partner, I lost my planner – my director. David had taken over our daily schedules since 1999. He was a planner. He planned trips and what to do every day. He was always thinking ahead. I never had to – I just gave my opinion when he asked. In fact, when we dated, I nicknamed him "A Man With A Plan."

That has all changed. There is no plan, except the big one – someday, I will see the Lord face to face and David again in heaven. In the meantime, I need to live for the Lord with a plan.

MAN MAKES PLANS, BUT THE LORD DIRECTS HIS STEPS, — PROVERBS 16:9.

So, do I want to volunteer or work part-time? How much time can I give my grandchildren? Direct my steps, Lord. I started thinking about where I would like to spend my new gift of time and decided to volunteer at a nursing home.

It was fun to stop at a nursing home and find out they had an opening for someone to teach Bible on Mondays. I worked at this twice a month for a while. I met wonderful people and enjoyed the time there.

As I continued to walk through life without David, grieving waves crashed at different times. One evening, I was congested from a winter cold. It was in the wonderful week between Christmas and the New Year. With my head feeling full, I started crying out to God. I let the tears flow and multiplied the congestion from the cold into a full-blown avalanche trying to push forth from inside my head. Finally, I shouted through the window, looking up to the heavens for any sign of life.

"Lord, Please – Please – Please – Please let me see David!"

I slowly made my way back to the sofa, closed my eyes and wept for a while. Trusting God's love, I gently peeked through the fog of tears, and the slits in my eyelids allowing sight, ever so slowly, to reveal no one else in the room. David wasn't visible. My already full head swayed back and forth with my reality. I steadied it with my hands, wiped my tears and shuffled into the bedroom.

I decided to sit in a comfy chair to play a video game – my escape. It actually has three, little, colored germs and the player throws pills to kill them. When David was in the middle of his battle, I pretended to be killing cancer cells with each victory in the game. I played it for an hour because falling asleep wasn't an option. An hour later, my head began to bob back and forth and I believed my body would allow me to sleep.

I ventured to bed and, after finding nothing of humor to watch on TV, darkened the room and prayed for our children and grandchildren. Then, I apologized to God for not accepting His will. I apologized for crying out to please see David. I accepted His forgiveness and thanked Him that He knows my heart. My lids closed over my puffy eyes and I gracefully fell into sleep.

As I awoke the next morning and greeted the beautiful sunrise, my mind slowly awakened to the reality that I had been with David.

While I dreamt, David was with me in our home. We hugged and spoke a few words. I laid my head on his chest. I had wanted to since March but the inflammation of the cancer cells had caused pressure there, so I hadn't found that comfort for the entire time he was sick. He pulled me close and our embrace filled all the longing I'd had since May. I asked him about heaven and he said he couldn't tell me much yet. And, there was his smile. He was so happy and so happy to see me, too. We looked around together, as voices filled the room and we watched our family. Wonderful, comforting, and as amazing as a warm embrace should be, I accepted God's covering of peace.

BUT HOPE THAT IS SEEN IS NO HOPE AT ALL. BUT IF WE HOPE FOR WHAT WE DO NOT YET HAVE, WE WAIT FOR IT PATIENTLY.
— ROMANS 8:24B-25

SEVENTEEN

A Gift From God

My trip to Florida in February was nice. I visited a friend near Jacksonville and then Sue, Bill's wife, joined me in Pompano Beach. I love the smell of Florida because it is a reminder of David. Packing was difficult, because there he was asking if I'd washed the white shirt he wanted to take or had I packed the phone charger.

I can see his smile as he nudged me to a shorter line through security at the airport and then his eyes rolling as they wanded him. Was it his belt buckle? I don't remember what it was, but he was picked out of line more than once. And then we waited. He always liked getting to the airport early – two hours usually – so we played cards or read books and waited. Once, we got on an earlier flight because we were so early – *oh, he was fun to travel with*! Often, if something was announced, like strong winds upon arrival, David would get another look on his face.

"This is not good," he'd say.

"Hon, don't say something if it doesn't encourage me, okay? Flying is difficult enough without you adding your concern to mine."

"You are right," he said.

And, he never did again.

That was another thing I loved about him. If something didn't feel right to me, David wouldn't do it again. He remembered what I liked and didn't like. I never had to ask him twice – even though he did need to mention my "slurping" soup more than once. I forgot that I did that until he mentioned it again.

Standing in Stein Mart in Florida I could hear him telling me to try something on and see him handing me a blouse. "Hon, try this." But he was not there. He loved to shop and help me pick out outfits. I could almost smell him as I walked the floor. I closed my eyes and drank it in – enjoying the sweet memory of his life as the tears began.

I visited our old condo, unit 412, and remembered when we bought it and worked hard on removing the grass cloth wallpaper. We were a mess that day, covered in paper and melted glue. We spent a lot of time picking out the right furniture, but the best part was the balcony. David would spend every evening after dinner sitting on the balcony watching the ocean and stars. He became inebriated on ocean breezes and moonlight and would slowly stumble back in and head for bed.

When Sue and I saw it, the new owner had changed the unit so much that I didn't shed a tear. I was expecting to cry out of a desire to be back in the unit with David and all I felt was that David and my unit were gone. It was actually easier to see it changed.

In March, I sought out a professional counselor to help me resolve the guilt I had been carrying since David's illness. She helped me realize that a lot of my sadness centered on guilt of what I thought I did wrong when David was sick.

Had I done everything I could?

If we had treated the discomfort in his chest earlier would it have made a difference?

Could I have done more to ease his pain?

She gave me a pearl of wisdom: the guilt I was carrying wasn't from God. If I believed I did a lot of wrong things trying to help David during the weeks of his illness, then I was saying God's grace was not sufficient. Living with *if only* or *what if* or *I should have* was cured now. I can accept that God gave me His grace and it was sufficient to minister to David as God would want – and as David needed – because God is sufficient. Not because Mary is – she can't be!

Now, I look at those five weeks as a gift from God – a gift to both of us to walk through a time of illness, but also a time of refining in both of our lives and we saw Christ at every turn.

When the hospital said there were no private rooms available – He opened one up so I could stay the night. Then, one of those nights he had pain in his chest from the blood clot and I was there to call the nurse and help him sit up for relief. How about how He opened the appointment for his PET scan? Or, how He set up doctor appointments – especially with Dr. McCall opening the radiation department just for us on a Saturday?

The Lord did so much for both of us. I thank Him for choosing me to be his wife and allowing me the grace to walk through those five weeks alongside him – allowing me to watch His servant deepen his love for Him and become accountable to Him. As his body failed him, David's heart grew and his love for God grew. He somehow started walking in heaven long before May 2nd.

Years ago, another friend Sue and I began talking on the phone every Saturday morning, to be accountable to each other. We talk about how we're doing in our relationship with Christ, our family, our friends, and our bodies.

In early March, I awoke from a good sleep. I opened the shades, looked out through the dark tree branches at a foggy, rainy morning, climbed back under the covers and called her. Toward the end of the conversation, I sensed something. My spirit sensed that David was in the room – I didn't mention it to Sue but decided to finish our conversation.

After we hung up, I made myself comfortable under the covers and asked God what it was that I sensed. My right arm was lying outside the covers, over the center of my body and I felt pressure on it. I closed my eyes and remembered all the times we would fall asleep together. David loved to snuggle up next to me and place his right arm across my right arm as he pulled me close to him. The pressure on my right arm increased and I remembered something that started when we were dating. David would call on rainy mornings and say that these were the times he missed being married. He loved to snuggle on a rainy morning and try to stay in bed as long as possible. We frequently did get a chance in our marriage to let rainy mornings linger with us snuggling in bed.

"If anything happens to either of us, this is what I would miss the most – snuggling together," he would often say.

That day, I lay there enjoying the presence of love and my arm became filled with goose bumps – just that arm. It was awesome. I basked in God's presence in my life and the union He had given David and I as husband and wife. We will always be united.

As tears started to stream down my cheeks, I asked the Lord if they were tears of joy or sadness and He answered by asking me not to analyze the moment.

So, I just soaked in the moment – I lay there remembering all the good night snuggles and good morning embraces until the tears stopped and the pressure left.

I wasn't just missing David, I was missing my life with him. I missed going to restaurants with him. I missed eating dinner with him. I missed having our day planned together. I missed my best friend calling and me calling him with every bit of "news" of the day. I loved when he would say "I know you don't pay attention to the news, or even like it, but something happened today you need to know about." Then, he would give me the latest. He kept me informed.

I missed so much of that wonderful man in my life – he was my friend, my confidant, my counselor, my golfing partner, my jokester, my lover, my companion, my encourager, my sounding board, my solid rock, oh – the list is endless.

I believe I was hugged by God *and* David that morning. I know that my Redeemer lives and that David G. Bulthuis lives. I am a woman truly blessed.

HOPE DEFERRED MAKES THE HEART SICK, BUT A LONGING FULFILLED IS A TREE OF LIFE. — PROVERBS 13:12

EPILOGUE

Lessons Learned

It is important to me that I begin this chapter with a comment on lessons. Even though the lessons have been learned, I sometimes revert back to old behaviors. The good news is that each year, I see more and more victory. Until heaven, I will continue to be a work in progress.

Reaching Out

Oh, how I have learned to be able to say I need help. The first time I thought of seeing a professional for assistance, I heard lies of "only crazy people need help" and "once you have seen a professional psychologist, you are labeled," which I have come to believe are the enemy's way of keeping us in bondage. The Truth, that I have found, is to have a teachable spirit. Knowing no one has it all together, we can accept our need for working on our issues.

> "For always there will be greater and lesser persons than yourself."
> — *Desiderata*

I WILL INSTRUCT YOU AND TEACH YOU IN THE WAY YOU SHOULD GO; I WILL COUNSEL YOU AND WATCH OVER YOU. — PSALM 32:8

Why would God instruct us if we already had all the answers?

Reaching out for answers when you are facing questions, anxieties, problems, losses, changes, sadness, loneliness or feelings of inferiority is the beginning of healing. Whether it was a professional appointment, prayer time with a friend, a book or a class, I am so grateful that I reached out – and continue to reach out – for answers.

Judgment & Respect

One of the prayer schools I attended taught me about judgment and respect. I had no idea I was so judgmental until I studied it. The book that helped me study judgments was called *How To Stop The Pain* by Dr. James Richards. This book taught me that we can observe others but as soon as we decide *why* others do something, we enter into judgment of them and/or their actions. I still have to work hard at observing others and not going further with my thoughts. It is a battle, because I have become very entrenched in my old way of judging – but it is doable, with the help of the Holy Spirit. I celebrate every small victory – taking ownership for my thoughts, taking every thought captive. Before studying this, my mind ran wild. I thought I knew what everyone else needed to get better or to solve their problem and I had the answer.

I learned that I would judge people and their situations and then I would be judged by them. It is a vicious cycle. In order to get out of it, I began by taking responsibility for past judgments – first of all to God. I had to take responsibility for my past attitude toward God – I used to entertain thoughts like "if I were God…" as though I knew better than the Creator of the Universe. I love to spend time at the ocean because it puts my size into perspective and I begin to retain thoughts of how *huge* God is. I need that. I also need to remember that I may not have a solution for others. Just because something worked for me or something blessed me, I need to remember that God has a unique road for all of us and I may not understand what you are handling or what He is teaching you.

DO NOT JUDGE OR YOU TOO WILL BE JUDGED. FOR IN THE SAME WAY YOU JUDGE OTHERS, YOU WILL BE JUDGED, AND WITH THE MEASURE YOU USE, IT WILL BE MEASURED TO YOU. — MATTHEW 7:1-2

I also realized I was judging myself as the savior, taking responsibility to fix others – especially if I thought they needed help. God has taught me to get off of His throne and trust He will take care of others. As a nurturer, and especially as a mother, it is really difficult to step out of the thoughts of what I need to do for someone. But, by His grace and my constant pleading to Him for help, I know it is do-able!

The book that changed my relationship with my mom was called *A Tribute and a Promise* by Dennis Rainey. My mom had raised us with a lot of fear and a lot of negativity. Controlling 12 children must have been some task, but, I seemed to focus on the negative aspects of her personality and parenting and became negative myself. I told myself I would never treat children like she treated us, yet that is a judgment and I did reap what I had sown. Judgment on myself – and I became negative. As I was working on this aspect of my personality, I needed to glean a lot of fears. My fears were connected to so much of my personality.

When I read the *Tribute* book, I was studying the commandment to honor your parents "so all will go well with you." I wanted all to go well with me and asked the Lord to help me. It took almost a year. He would remind me of something sweet about my mom – something I had not thought of in years. I would write thoughts, as I remembered them one at a time, on the computer. After a year, I had compiled enough and talked to my husband about honoring her with a tribute at a family dinner. My parents took all the adult children and spouses out to dinner to celebrate Christmas. Christmas of 2001, as we were finishing the meal, I asked if I could say a few words. We were in a small, private room at a nice restaurant and you could hear a pin drop. My knees became weak and I searched David's face for encouragement – and with a nod of his head, I turned to face my siblings and parents and began to read out loud the following:

A Tribute to My Mom

Every time I smell home made bread, coffee cake and stew, I slowly drift to warm memories of you in the kitchen. Every time I smell Emeraude, I think of a little girl admiring her mom. Every time I smell Gardenias, I smile knowing it is your favorite flower. Every time I see a rose, I remember the fragrance and beauty of your garden.

I loved watching you love your mom. I learned respect for parents every time we went to grandma's. Visions of her white horse on the mantle flood my mind as I joyfully remember visiting her often. I would watch you speak to her, listen to her and learn from her.

I can still see us playing with your hair from the back seat on the way home from grandma's house as we pulled into Cock Robin's for ice cream.

I learned devotion to Our Lord by watching you pray. I enjoyed keeping quiet on Good Friday and was taught how to fast through your example.

You struggled to keep us afloat after dad died, and I learned how to work hard to pay bills along with how important we all were to you.

I learned the value of a dollar when you got me a job at National, because it paid more than my job at the Northlake Deli.

My love for dancing was passed on from yours. I can still see you glide across the dance floor with dad. I was so proud to be your daughter.

You loved us best by cooking and cleaning up after us; You could do more with a pound of ground beef than anyone I have ever met.

You gave of yourself freely, denying yourself in order for us to survive. I wonder just how many nights of sleep you lost taking care of all of us. You took care of us so well, we never went hungry or without clothing, even though you didn't have any money.

Your homemade remedies I still use – like Vicks and tea bags.

It must have been hard for you to put our dog to sleep and put up with all of our questions and I probably don't now half of all you did as our mom.

I thank God for choosing you to mother me, for you played an extremely important role in my life and gave me the best support you could, throughout even the most difficult times.

Your example prepared me to parent my children through very lean years and I am forever grateful. You didn't always understand my choices, but listened and helped, doing all you could to show your love.

So today, mom, I want to recognize your love and say thank you. From the bottom of my heart. I thank God for you.

Mary, 2001

I would look up every few sentences to notice her head in a dropped position. She looked like a little girl. So frail, so humble, so wounded by life that she didn't know how to look up when someone was saying something nice. She didn't say anything afterward. Dad came up to me and thanked me.

She went to heaven about 15 months later, at the age of 84 and I found this tribute in a frame in the center of her dresser. I like to think she read it often.

Boundaries

When I first read the wonderful book by Townsend and Cloud, I decided to try boundaries with my children. I announced that they were going to be responsible for more things – age appropriate responsibilities. For instance, they were all capable of waking themselves up after a night's sleep. I would help them get an alarm clock, if they needed one, but I would no longer be responsible for them in the morning. One son asked if I could just make a lot of noise using the bathroom, as it was right next to his bedroom. I said no! It took a little while, but they got the hang of taking on some responsibility. They all learned how to do laundry while in high school. They were capable and we all had busy schedules.

Now, working on boundaries with adults was different and slow going. I remember when I first began speaking to my mom with boundaries. She was praising one sibling in front of the rest of us, but not just to let us know he was a good son, but to also instill guilt that we didn't do for her what he did.

"Mom, are you trying to make us feel guilty?" I said softly. This was not usually put into words in my family.

"Yes," she replied with a smirk.

"Oh," I replied, "I didn't know if I mentioned it to you, but I don't do guilt anymore."

"Well," she answered, "our relationship is based on guilt."

"If that is so, then I guess we don't have a relationship."

The room was quiet – the siblings didn't know if they should laugh or be shocked that someone had brought out in the open what we all felt for so many years. It is important to set boundaries with love – with soft words of respect. Boundaries and consequences are a wonderful way to have relationships. David taught me that love was unconditional because it was God in us that could love others. But, he would say, relationships are conditional. Both parties have to do their part. I used to work hard on my part and tried to keep both of the sides of the relationship working. Now I let others be responsible for their part of our relationship. Wahoo! Freedom!

Our Strengths are Our Weaknesses

David said this often. We are all gifted – physically, emotionally and spiritually. Once we recognize our giftedness, we can take it to extremes. My example is, in my giftedness of loving prayer, if someone is hurting I immediately want to pray with them. Some people are not ready for healing and I step in too soon. I want to help people and *fix* their pain, especially if it is some pain I have personally experienced. Now, that sounds like a good thing, but I have offended people instead of helping them.

There were many days that I heard a teaching that sounded so good to me, but before absorbing it totally, I would purchase it for three other people. That is like saying "You have the same problem I have."

God often says to me in a thought, "I wanted you to hear this – not think of who else it would bless." How humbling! It is so easy for me to see other's issues than look at my own.

WHY DO YOU LOOK AT THE SPECK OF SAWDUST IN YOUR BROTHER'S EYE AND PAY NO ATTENTION TO THE PLANK IN YOUR OWN EYE? HOW CAN YOU SAY TO YOUR BROTHER, "LET ME TAKE THE SPECK OUT OF YOUR EYE," WHEN ALL THE TIME THERE IS A PLANK IN YOUR OWN EYE? YOU HYPOCRITE, FIRST TAKE THE PLANK OUT OF YOUR OWN EYE, AND THEN YOU WILL SEE CLEARLY TO REMOVE THE SPECK FROM YOUR BROTHER'S EYES. — MATTHEW 7:3-5

Respond or React?

I first heard about this choice in CoDA, but first experienced someone who lived it through David. As I asked him a question, I awaited his reply – or reaction – thinking he would begin speaking before I was finished talking. Conversations where you have an answer before the other person is through speaking were common in my life. In fact, I learned to have thoughts, while someone else was talking, about how I would answer their words – or how I could compare my experiences to what they were sharing. This didn't allow me to focus on what they were saying. It is a self-focused way to converse.

The first time I noticed the difference between responding and reacting was out to dinner with David. I asked him a question. Nothing. Then, slowly, he repeated the question out loud. He was preparing a reply – responding. He actually thought about what I said after he heard it – not while hearing it – and prepared a response.

David recommended a book called *Boundaries* by Cloud and Townsend and it changed my life.

Respond, Don't React

When you react to something that someone says or does, you may have a problem with boundaries. If someone is able to cause havoc by doing or saying something, she is in control of you at that point, and your boundaries are lost. When you respond, you remain in control, with options and choices.

If you feel yourself reacting, step away and regain control of yourself so family members can't force you to do or say something you do not want to do or say and something that violates your separateness. When you have kept your boundaries, choose the best option. The difference between responding and reacting is choice. When you are reacting, they are in control. When you respond, you are.

Learn to Love in Freedom and Responsibility, Not in Guilt

The best boundaries are loving ones. The person who has to remain forever in a protective mode is losing out on love and freedom. Boundaries in no way mean to stop loving. They mean the opposite: you are gaining freedom to love. It is good to sacrifice and deny yourself for the sake of others. But you need boundaries to make that choice.

Practice purposeful giving to increase your freedom. Sometimes people who are building boundaries feel that to do someone a favor is codependent. Nothing is farther from the truth. Doing good for someone, when you freely choose to do it, is boundary enhancing. Codependents are not doing good; they are allowing evil because they are afraid. [5]

As I tried to learn this concept, I gradually noticed that my response was always more beneficial to others than my reaction. I react for many reasons. The usual reason is to defend myself, my position or my belief. The most noticeable reaction is getting excited, or panicky inside due to an uncomfortable conversation.

There are many individuals in my life that I struggle to stay in relationships with – but I know God loves them and has strategically placed them in my life for me to show them His love. I do try to love them with healthy boundaries – taking care of myself and not allowing abuse. But, conversations come up where I feel misunderstood or where I believe they are wrong, according to what I have learned in the Bible.

As my spirit starts to get panicky inside over the conversation, if I react, I try to *fix* them. The lesson learned is that I don't have that power. My words may fall on deaf ears. I am an intercessor – a prayer warrior. God keeps reminding me to respond – if I get panicky inside, to immediately say "I'll have to pray about that." That should be the end of that conversation at that time. God may bring it up again another day, but if I'm panicky inside, I am not in a place to have a discussion.

I'm learning to love people where they are without reacting to any issues that may stir inside me while they talk. I realize that I allow others to *take away* some of my peace if I focus on a reaction instead of a response.

Conviction, Not Condemnation

Blind sided – is that the phrase – when you are totally shocked as someone verbally abuses you? Once I understood verbal abuse, I had to learn boundaries. As I tried to enforce them in my life, I was tested. For years, I failed the test.

When I read a letter from a relative – a letter containing examples of many things that I had done wrong in my life, of ways I had caused others to exemplify poor behavior and ways I had ruined other's lives – my body began to shake. My first thoughts were, "Oh, my – this is full of hatred." I cried for days if the letter came to mind. I had torn it up as soon as I finished reading it and when I found out a copy was sent to my mom, I walked around in a soft fog of who I was and who I trusted.

I tried to deal with the accusation that I was a terrible relative.

It reminded me of the Amalekites [I Samuel 30:1]. They are known Biblically for attacking others when they are in a weak place – like the men had gone off to war, so they attacked the women and children left in camp. Well, this attack came while I was trying to put the pieces of our family life together after just leaving my husband. I don't know if I was ever weaker than when I was a single mom with four small children leaving an abusive marriage.

Several years later, a school friend was arguing with another friend. I entered the conversation and she began to holler at me. I remember listening to her and thinking this wasn't really about me, but believing I did not give her enough friend time. So I made a point to visit this person with a small gift for several years. I chose to give them some attention.

I tried to deal with the accusation that I was a terrible friend.

Years later, when beginning my second marriage, a good sister-in-Christ came over while I was home alone. Upon entering my home, she began to *vomit* her accusations on me of what a terrible Christian friend I was. I remember listening for a while, apologizing and then leading her to the door while mentally in another fog. Who was this woman and why does she hate me so much?

I tried to deal with the accusation that I was a terrible Christian.

When someone at church asked for prayer for a sibling, I put out the prayer request, as I have always believed the more prayers fighting the battle, the better chances for victory. When this person called and *vomited* piercing words about what a terrible person I was for telling anyone about the prayer request, I began to shake and weep inside. I didn't understand.

I tried to deal with the accusation that I was a terrible confidant.

Now, in their defense, I do not do everything right. God is continuing to refine me and I have a lot to learn. But, I am not a terrible relative, friend, sister-in-Christ or confidant.

These examples have one thing in common – the individual did not talk to me in a loving voice – they attacked me when I was totally unaware that there was anything wrong. The Bible teaches us to speak the Truth in love. I've learned that these attacks are not from the individuals – people are used by evil to forward evil's kingdom of condemnation in our lives. Most times, the people don't even know they are being used. They are shouting/vomiting out of their own pain and hurt.

The Good News: Some lessons are learned.

As I was *vomited on* again years later, and I hung up the phone to lay on the floor and cry for hours, the Lord encouraged me to call a friend. I wept on the phone to her. "Please pray for me," I managed to say between sobs. She prayed for me and as my spirit received her prayers, I recognized this as an attack by the enemy, not the person who had spoken the words. That person was in pain.

When we do wrong the Holy Spirit convicts us to bring us to

repentance. If we feel condemnation, we are taught otherwise in the Bible.

"THERE IS THEREFORE, NOW, NO CONDEMNATION FOR THOSE WHO BELONG TO CHRIST JESUS." — ROMANS 8:1

Conviction, yes – condemnation, no.

There is a big difference.

The Holy Spirit is gentle and loving, and speaks the Truth in Love [Ephesians 4:15]. Do not receive others' issues or pain – be responsible for your own and ask forgiveness, if necessary, but if someone shouts/hollers/vomits speech or harsh words in any form, you can walk away and pray for them.

I love to quote Joyce Meyers: "Hurt people hurt people."

So, this final time of having *vomit* spewed on me from someone else's pain, I didn't receive it. After shedding sufficient tears of repentance for my part in the situation, and asking the Lord to allow them to understand my heart, I prayed for them. Then, I picked myself up and attended an afternoon event I was supposed to go to with a smile on my face. The Truth in my friend's words encouraged me to fight the battle with a smile.

May we all know who we are fighting and take our stand, no matter how weak we are, to only receive conviction – not condemnation. Our Lord loves us too much for us to stay on the floor in tears of condemnation.

He will pick us up.

WHEN WE LOOK TO HIM, OUR FACES ARE RADIANT, THEY ARE NEVER COVERED IN SHAME! — PSALM 34:5

Wait for Them to Ask/And They Shall Receive

As I try to catch myself before I say it, it still slips out of my mouth. I try to retract it – words of *instruction* or *wisdom*. An old episode of *Andy Griffith* depicted Barney trying to *fix* Opie's issue with math at school and it frustrated Andy. I identified with Barney – seeing something that was someone else's responsibility and thinking I needed to fix it. Stepping in without being asked my opinion. And, I saw my children, especially, like Andy – loving me but being frustrated.

This lesson I would really like to learn. Waiting for people to ask before giving any wisdom. Only being responsible for what I should be responsible for or concerned with. As David said, "Our strengths are our weaknesses." Sometimes I do have good advice – but it still is not something I should give out before the individual asks for it. If I give it out, in advance, it sounds like I think I know better. I believe it is one of the avenues of entrance pride has into my brain and relationships.

I think God wants us to ask, also. He has all the answers but gave us free will. He wants us to love Him freely and in asking Him, we are trusting Him to go to His storehouse and provide. Asking shows our dependence on Him and His responsibility to step in as His Word promises.

ASK AND YOU SHALL RECEIVE AND YOUR JOY WILL BE COMPLETE.
— JOHN 16:24

This *asking* issue not only demonstrates our need for His wisdom, I think it also demonstrates His gift of free will. He won't force us to do the right thing.

The same day I was watching *Andy Griffith*, as I changed channels, my eyes were *slimed* by sexual images on some channels that I had never wanted to see. I had a choice to remain on the sexually explicit channels that would continue to slime my mind with demonic use of the human body, or to change the channel and surrender to what God would want my eyes to focus on.

WHATEVER IS RIGHT, WHATEVER IS PURE, WHATEVER IS LOVELY, WHATEVER IS ADMIRABLE – IF ANYTHING IS EXCELLENT OR PRAISEWORTHY – THINK ABOUT SUCH THINGS. — PHILIPPIANS 4:8

I have learned to pray for the entertainment industry as I ask the Lord to cleanse me from anything that does not bow down to Jesus Christ that has been exposed to my eyes. But, I have to ask God to help me. I cannot think of what is right without His help. On my own, I would be drawn to be entertained by what this world offers, which strips away from the purity, respect and holiness of our bodies.

The Power of the Tongue

Scripture says that "Life and death are in the power of the tongue." When I saw the book *Me and My Big Mouth* by Joyce Meyer on the shelf in Family Bookstore, I picked it up and wrapped it as a present for David to give to me one Christmas. I thought everyone would enjoy the joke. They did. It then sat on the shelf for several years until the Holy Spirit nudged me to read it. I have now read it over five times – each time trying to grasp what changes I can make with my mouth.

I have seen life come out of the mouth – our grandchildren smile when we give them praise; tears come to David's eyes as I practice my speech to women at Church; a son try harder at baseball as we cheer from the sidelines; friends *light up* when I compliment them and police officers' countenance melt as I say "thank you for serving."

And, I have witnessed death come out of the tongue – the evil one has even used my mouth to speak condemnation on family members, friends, or to go along with gossip or laughter at other people. I've even allowed the use of my tongue to put myself down.

Thanks to the grace of God, no more. I am learning to keep my mouth shut until I know that what will come out of it will be said with love and will be life-giving.

RECKLESS WORDS PIERCE LIKE A SWORD, BUT THE TONGUE OF THE WISE BRINGS HEALING. — PROVERBS 12:18

My favorite example of practicing this lesson was while studying Godly submission. I was trying to understand respect for my husband in the Biblical calling.

David was sitting, watching TV in a recliner, and I was peeling potatoes. Hundreds of thoughts were circling around in my head – negative thoughts about him.

"Do you know that I am having many thoughts right now about what you do wrong?" I said to him.

"No," he said, "I'm not having any thoughts right now. Do you want to tell me about them?"

"NO", I said emphatically, "I don't want to even voice them. I want to focus on what I love about you instead. Would you pray for me?"

He said he would – and I learned that the battle is often in my head. It is not that David did everything right, none of us do. But, I can choose to focus on what he did right instead of what he may not do exactly as I would like it.

After that day, I learned the value of keeping my mouth shut and praying instead of complaining. I ask God each day to guide the words of my mouth.

Final Thoughts on Hope

My ideas of Hope – the golden thread that connects us to joy.

Hope – the life preserver that keeps us afloat when we are being rocked back and forth in a storm.

Hope – the smile or words you give to another to recognize their situation and let them know you made it through something similar.

Hope – the silver lining to a dark cloud.

According to the dictionary:

hope |hōp| noun

The feeling that what is wanted can be had; or that events will turn out for the best.

What is wanted can be had – because what is wanted is love, peace and joy. All of these are by-products of a relationship with Jesus. They can be had. I am living proof.

JESUS ANSWERED, "I AM THE WAY, THE TRUTH AND THE LIFE."
— JOHN 14:6

Events will turn out for the best.

AND WE KNOW THAT IN ALL THINGS GOD WORKS FOR THE GOOD OF THOSE WHO LOVE HIM, WHO HAVE BEEN CALLED ACCORDING TO HIS PURPOSES. — ROMANS 8:28

Every breath we take is hope. Every breath brings life into our bodies. And, when that life is connected to our Maker, Our Lord and Savior, Jesus Christ, His Father and the Holy Spirit, it is truly life-giving. It penetrates to every cell with new life.

He created us and loves us. Loves us so much He died to bring us into a relationship with Him so we can enjoy eternity with Him. Can you imagine loving that much?

Believe we can't even imagine what He has planned for those who love Him and follow His Words. He gave us instructions on how to make life work on earth. As long as we study the instruction manual, life is good.

Hope is knowing – believing – in a Good God who loves us. Believing the same God who created us, who even decided to send us to earth, is at work for our good right now.

My life story is a testimony to a God of Love. I receive His Love and look for more each day.

Hope Revealed!

-❧ ❧ ❧-

"For I know the plans I have for you," declares the Lord, "plans to prosper you and not to harm you, plans to give you hope and a future." — Jeremiah 29:11

REALITY & SUPPORT

What About You?

This closing section offers information and real-life statistics about some of the challenges I faced. It also suggests possible resources where you can obtain help should you be facing a similar situation. This information is by no means exhaustive, but hopefully it will encourage you to take that next step to reclaim peace in your life. I spent far too many years of my life denying that the circumstances surrounding me could be changed.

The presence of God in my life gave me the inner strength to move forward and allowed me to seek the knowledge, information, and counsel to change those circumstances. I learned first-hand that knowledge is power and that seeking and accepting help is the noble and the right thing to do.

Domestic Violence [6]

Domestic violence is the willful intimidation, physical assault, battery, sexual assault, and/or other abusive behavior perpetrated by an intimate partner against another.

It is an epidemic affecting individuals in every community, regardless of age, economic status, race, religion, nationality or educational background. Violence against women is often accompanied by emotionally abusive and controlling behavior, and thus is part of a systematic pattern of dominance and control.

Domestic violence results in physical injury, psychological trauma, and sometimes death. The consequences of domestic violence can cross generations and truly last a lifetime.

- *One in every four women will experience domestic violence in her lifetime.*
- *An estimated 1.3 million women are victims of physical assault by an intimate partner each year.*
- *85% of domestic violence victims are women.*
- *Historically, females have been most often victimized by someone they knew.*
- *Females who are 20-24 years of age are at the greatest risk of nonfatal intimate partner violence.*
- *Most cases of domestic violence are never reported to the police.*

CHILDREN WHO WITNESS DOMESTIC VIOLENCE

- *Witnessing violence between one's parents or caretakers is the strongest risk factor of transmitting violent behavior from one generation to the next.*
- *Boys who witness domestic violence are twice as likely to abuse their own partners and children when they become adults.*
- *30% to 60% of perpetrators of intimate partner violence also abuse children in the household.*

SEXUAL ASSAULT AND STALKING

- *One in 6 women and one in 33 men have experienced an attempted or completed rape.*
- *Nearly 7.8 million women have been raped by an intimate partner at some point in their lives.*
- *Sexual assault or forced sex occurs in approximately 40-45% of battering relationships.*
- *One in 12 women and one in 45 men have been stalked in their lifetime.*
- *81% of women stalked by a current or former intimate partner are also physically assaulted by that partner; 31% are also sexually assaulted by that partner.*

HOMICIDE AND INJURY

- *Almost one-third of female homicide victims that are reported in police records are killed by an intimate partner.*

- *In 70-80% of intimate partner homicides, no matter which partner was killed, the man physically abused the woman before the murder.*

- *Less than one-fifth of victims reporting an injury from intimate partner violence sought medical treatment following the injury.*

- *Intimate partner violence results in more than 18.5 million mental health care visits each year.*

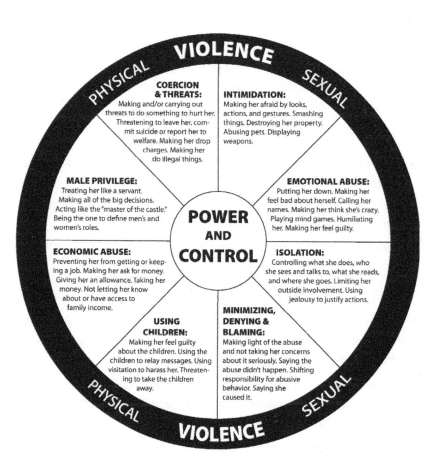

ECONOMIC IMPACT

- *The cost of intimate partner violence exceeds $5.8 billion each year, $4.1 billion of which is for direct medical and mental health services.*

- *Victims of intimate partner violence lost almost eight million days of paid work because of the violence perpetrated against them by current or former husbands, boyfriends and dates. This loss is the equivalent of more than 32,000 full-time jobs and almost 5.6 million days of household productivity as a result of violence.*

- *There are 16,800 homicides and $2.2 million (medically treated) injuries due to intimate partner violence annually, which costs $37 billion.*

REPORTING RATES

- *Domestic violence is one of the most chronically underreported crimes.*

- *Only approximately one-quarter of all physical assaults, one-fifth of all rapes, and one-half of all stalkings perpetuated against females by intimate partners are reported to the police.*

PROTECTION ORDERS

- *Approximately 20% of the 1.5 million people who experience intimate partner violence annually obtain civil protection orders.*

- *Approximately one-half of the orders obtained by women against intimate partners who physically assaulted them were violated.*

- *More than two-thirds of the restraining orders against intimate partners who raped or stalked the victim were violated.*

STATE DOMESTIC VIOLENCE LAWS

States differ on the type of relationship that qualifies under domestic violence laws. Most states require the perpetrator and victim to be current or former spouses, living together, or have a child in common.

A significant number of states include current or former dating relationships in domestic violence laws. Delaware, Montana and South Carolina specifically exclude same-sex relationships in their domestic violence laws.

To find more information on the domestic violence laws in your state, please visit www.womenslaw.org.

Support

For more information, please visit the website of the National Coalition Against Domestic Violence at www.ncadv.org.

To get help, please call:

THE NATIONAL DOMESTIC VIOLENCE HOTLINE at 1-800-799-7233

THE NATIONAL SEXUAL ASSAULT HOTLINE AT 1-800-656-4673

THE NATIONAL TEEN DATING ABUSE HOTLINE AT 1-866-331-9474

Source: National Coalition Against Domestic Violence

Codependence

An Excerpt from Codependent No More *[7] by Melody Beattie*

WHAT'S CODEPENDENCY?

I have heard and read many definitions of codependency. In an article from the book Co-Dependency, An Emerging Issue, *Robert Subby wrote codependency is: "An emotional, psychological, and behavioral condition that develops as a result of an individual's prolonged exposure to, and practice of, a set of oppressive rules—rules which prevent the open expression of feeling as well as the direct discussion of personal and interpersonal problems."*

Earnie Larsen, another codependency specialist and a pioneer in that field, defines codependency as: "Those self-defeating, learned behaviors or character defects that result in a diminished capacity to initiate or to participate in loving relationships."

Some less professional definitions follow. "Codependency means," said one woman, "that I'm a caretaker." "Being codependent means I'm married to an alcoholic," responded one woman. "It also means I need to go to Al-Anon."

"Codependency," replied another, "means I'm up to my elbows in alcoholics."

"It means I'm always looking for someone to glob onto." "Codependency? It means I know any man I'm attracted to, fall in love with, or marry will be chemically dependent or have some other equally serious problem."

"Codependency," explained one person, "is knowing all your relationships will either go on and on the same way (painfully), or end the same way (disastrously). Or both."

171

There are almost as many definitions of codependency as there are experiences that represent it. In desperation (or perhaps enlightenment), some therapists have proclaimed: "Codependency is anything, and everyone is codependent." So, who's got the inside story? Which definition is accurate? A brief history of codependency will help answer this question.

A BRIEF HISTORY

The word codependency appeared on the treatment scene in the late seventies. I don't know who discovered it. Although several people may claim to have done so, the word emerged simultaneously in several different treatment centers in Minnesota, according to information from the office of Sondra Smalley, C.C.D.P., a licensed psychologist and a leader in the codependency field. Maybe Minnesota, the heartland of chemical dependency treatment and Twelve Step programs for compulsive disorders, discovered it.

Robert Subby and John Friel, in an article from the book <u>Co-Dependency, An Emerging Issue</u>, wrote: "Originally, it was used to describe the person or persons whose lives were affected as a result of their being involved with someone who was chemically dependent. The Co-dependent spouse or child or lover of someone who was chemically dependent was seen as having developed a pattern of coping with life that was not healthy, as a reaction to someone else's drug or alcohol abuse."

It was a new name for an old game. Professionals had long suspected something peculiar happened to people who were closely involved with chemically dependent people. Some research had been done on the subject, indicating a physical, mental, emotional, and spiritual condition similar to alcoholism seemed to appear in many nonalcoholic or non-chemically dependent people who were close to an alcoholic. Words (more jargon which would later become synonymous for codependent) surfaced to describe this phenomenon: co-alcoholic, nonalcoholic, para-alcoholic.

Codependents certainly felt the effects of codependency long before the word was coined. In the 1940s, after the birth of Alcoholics Anonymous, a group of people—primarily wives of alcoholics—formed self-help, support groups to deal with the ways their spouses' alcoholism affected them. They didn't know they would later be called codependents. They did know they had been directly affected by their mates' alcoholism. And, they were envious that alcoholics had a Twelve Step program to recover through. The wives also wanted a program. So they used the A.A. Twelve Step program, revised the A.A. Twelve Traditions, changed its name to Al-Anon, and it worked! Millions of people have since benefited from Al-Anon.

The basic thought then, and in 1979 when the word codependency emerged, was codependents (co-alcoholics or para-alcoholics) were people whose lives had become unmanageable as a result of living in a committed relationship with an alcoholic."

However, the definition for codependency has expanded since then. Professionals began to better understand the effects of the chemically dependent person on the family, and the effects of the family on the chemically dependent person. Professionals began to identify other problems such as overeating and undereating, gambling, and certain sexual behaviors. These compulsive disorders paralleled the compulsive disorder, or illness, of alcoholism. Professionals also began to notice many people in close relationships with these compulsive people developed patterns of reacting and coping that resembled the coping patterns of people in relationships with alcoholics. Something peculiar had happened to these families, too.

As professionals began to understand codependency better, more groups of people appeared to have it: adult children of alcoholics; people in relationships with emotionally or mentally disturbed persons; people in relationships with chronically ill people; parents of children with behavior problems; people in relationships with irresponsible people; professionals—nurses, social workers, and others in "helping" occupations. Even recovering alcoholics and addicts noticed they were codependent and perhaps had been long before becoming chemically dependent. Codependents started cropping up everywhere.

When a codependent discontinued his or her relationship with a troubled person, the codependent frequently sought another troubled person and repeated the codependent behaviors with that new person. These behaviors, or coping mechanisms, seemed to prevail throughout the codependent's life—if that person didn't change these behaviors.

Was it safe to assume codependency was triggered through relationships with people who have serious illnesses, behavior problems, or destructive compulsive disorders? Alcoholism in the family helped create codependency, but many other circumstances seemed to produce it, also.

One fairly common denominator was having a relationship, personally or professionally, with troubled, needy, or dependent people. But a second, more common denominator seemed to be the unwritten, silent rules that usually develop in the immediate family and set the pace for relationships. These rules prohibit discussion about problems; open expression of feelings; direct, honest communication; realistic expectations, such as being human, vulnerable, or imperfect; selfishness; trust in other people and one's self; playing and having fun; and rocking the delicately balanced family canoe through growth or change—however healthy and beneficial that movement might be. These rules are common to alcoholic family systems but can emerge in other families too.

Now, I return to an earlier question: Which definition of codependency is accurate? They all are. Some describe the cause, some the effects, some the overall condition, some the symptoms, some the patterns, and some the pain. Codependency either meant, or has come to mean, all the definitions listed earlier.

I'm not trying to confuse you. Codependency has a fuzzy definition because it is a gray, fuzzy condition. It is complex, theoretical, and difficult to completely define in one or two sentences.

Why all this fuss about a definition? Because I'm going to attempt the difficult—define codependent in one sentence. And, I want you to see the broader picture before I show you the narrower one. I hope this approach might help you identify codependency in yourself, if that identification is appropriate. Defining the problem is important because it helps determine the solution. Here, the solution is vital. It means feeling better. It means recovery.

So, here is my definition of a codependent:

A codependent person is one who has let another person's behavior affect him or her, and who is obsessed with controlling that person's behavior.

The other person might be a child, an adult, a lover, a spouse, a brother, a sister, a grandparent, a parent, a client, or a best friend. He or she could be an alcoholic, a drug addict, a mentally or physically ill person, a normal person who occasionally has sad feelings, or one of the people mentioned earlier.

But, the heart of the definition and recovery lies not in the other person—no matter how much we believe it does. It lies in ourselves, in the ways we have let other people's behavior affect us and in the ways we try to affect them: the obsessing, the controlling, the obsessive "helping," caretaking, low self-worth bordering on self-hatred, self-repression, abundance of anger and guilt, peculiar dependency on peculiar people, attraction to and tolerance for the bizarre, other-centeredness that *results in abandonment of self, communication problems, intimacy problems, and an ongoing whirlwind trip through the five-stage grief process.*

Is codependency an illness? Some professionals say codependency isn't a disease; they say it's a normal reaction to abnormal people.

Other professionals say codependency is a disease; it's a chronic, progressive illness. They suggest codependents want and need sick people around them to be happy in an unhealthy way. They say, for instance, the wife of an alcoholic needed to marry an alcoholic and chose him because she unconsciously thought he was an alcoholic. Furthermore, she needed him drinking and socking it to her to feel fulfilled.

This latter judgment may be overly harsh. I'm convinced codependents need less harshness in their lives. Other people have been hard enough on us. We have been hard enough on ourselves. Friends, we have suffered enough. We have been victimized by diseases and people. Each of us must decide what part we played in our victimization.

I don't know if codependency is or isn't an illness. I'm not an expert. But, to tell you what I believe, let me complete the brief history of Co-dependency which I started earlier in this chapter.

Although the first Al-Anon groups were formed in the 1940s, I am certain we could go back to the beginning of time and human relationships and find glimmers of codependent behavior. People have always had problems, and others have always cared for their troubled friends and relatives. People have likely been caught up with the problems of others since relationships began.

Codependency probably trailed man as he struggled through the remaining B.C. years, right up to "these generally wretched times of the twentieth century," as Morley Safer of 60 Minutes says. Ever since people first existed, they have been doing all the things we label "codependent." They have worried themselves sick about other people. They have tried to help in ways that didn't help. They have said yes when they meant no. They have tried to make other people see things their way. They have bent over backward to avoid hurting people's feelings and, in so doing, have hurt themselves. They have been afraid to trust their feelings. They have believed lies and then felt betrayed. They have wanted to get even and punish others. They have felt so angry they wanted to kill. They have struggled for their rights while other people said they didn't have any. They have worn sackcloth because they didn't believe they deserved silk.

Codependents have undoubtedly done good deeds too. By their nature, codependents are benevolent—concerned about and responsive to the needs of the world. As Thomas Wright writes in an article from the book <u>Co-Dependency, An Emerging Issue</u>, "I suspect codependents have historically attacked social injustice and fought for the rights of the underdog. Codependents want to help. I suspect they have helped. But they probably died thinking they didn't do enough and were feeling guilty.

"It is natural to want to protect and help the people we care about. It is also natural to be affected by and react to the problems of people around us. As a problem becomes more serious and remains unresolved, we become more affected and react more intensely to it."

The word react is important here. However you approach codependency, however you define it, and from whatever frame of reference you choose to diagnose and treat it, codependency is primarily a reactionary process. Codependents are reactionaries. They overreact. They under-react. But rarely do they act. They react to the problems, pains, lives, and behaviors of others. They react to their own problems, pains, and behaviors. Many codependent reactions are reactions to stress and uncertainty of living or growing up with alcoholism and other problems. It is normal to react to stress. It is not necessarily abnormal, but it is heroic and life-saving to learn how to not react and to act in more healthy ways. Most of us, however, need help to learn to do that.

Perhaps one reason some professionals call codependency a disease is because many codependents are reacting to an illness such as alcoholism.

Another reason codependency is called a disease is because it is progressive. As the people around us become sicker, we may begin to react more intensely. What began as a little concern may trigger isolation, depression, emotional or physical illness, or suicidal fantasies. One thing leads to another, and things get worse. Codependency may not be an illness, but it can make you sick. And, it can help the people around you stay sick.

Another reason codependency is called a disease is because Co-dependent behaviors—like many self-destructive behaviors—become habitual. We repeat habits without thinking. Habits take on a life of their own.

Whatever problem the other person has, codependency involves a habitual system of thinking, feeling, and behaving toward ourselves and others that can cause us pain. *Codependent behaviors or habits are self-destructive. We frequently react to people who are destroying themselves; we react by learning to destroy ourselves. These habits can lead us into, or keep us in, destructive relationships, relationships that don't work. These behaviors can sabotage relationships that may otherwise have worked. These behaviors can prevent us from finding peace and happiness with the most important person in our lives—ourselves. These behaviors belong to the only person each of us can control—the only person we can change—ourselves. These are our problems.*

Codependent No More, Beattie, Melody; Hazelden Foundation: Center City, MN, 1986, 1992

An Excerpt from Beyond Codependence [8] *by Melody Beattie*

THE GRATITUDE PRINCIPLE

Deprived thinking turns good things into less or nothing. Grateful thinking turns things into more.

Many years ago, when I started rebuilding a life shattered by my chemical use, I dreamt of getting married and raising a family. I also dreamt of owning a house, a beautiful home to be our little castle. I wanted some of the things other people had. I wanted "normal," whatever that was.

It looked like I was about to get it. I got married. I got pregnant. I had a baby girl. Now, all I needed was the home. We looked at all sorts of dream homes — big dream homes and in-between dream homes. The home we bought didn't turn out to be one of those, but it was the one we could afford.

It had been used as rental property for fifteen years, had been standing vacant for a year, and was three stories of broken windows and broken wood. Some rooms had ten layers of wallpaper on the walls. Some walls had holes straight through to the outdoors. The floors were covered with bright orange carpeting with large stains on it. And we didn't have money or skills to fix it. We had no money for windows, curtains, paint. We couldn't afford to furnish it. We had three stories of a dilapidated home, with a kitchen table, two chairs, a high chair, a bed, a crib, and two dressers, one of which had broken drawers.

About two weeks after we moved in, a friend stopped by. We stood talking on what would have been the lawn if grass had been growing there. My friend kept repeating how lucky I was and how nice it was to own your own home. But I didn't feel lucky,

---

and it didn't feel nice. I didn't know anyone else who owned a home like this.

I didn't talk much about how I felt, but each night while my husband and daughter slept, I tiptoed down to the living room, sat on the floor and cried. This became a ritual. When everyone was asleep, I sat in the middle of the floor thinking about everything I hated about the house, crying, and feeling hopeless. I did this for months. However legitimate my reaction may have been, it changed nothing.

A few times, in desperation, I tried to fix up the house, but nothing worked. The day before Thanksgiving I attempted to put some paint on the living and dining room walls. But layers of wallpaper started to peel off the minute I put paint on them. Another time, I ordered expensive wallpaper, trying to have faith I'd have the money to pay for it when it came. I didn't.

Then one evening, when I was sitting in the middle of the floor going through my wailing ritual, a thought occurred to me: Why don't I try gratitude?

At first I dismissed the idea. Gratitude was absurd. What could I possibly be grateful for? How could I? And why should I? Then, I decided to try anyway. I had nothing to lose. And I was getting sick of my whining.

I still wasn't certain what to be grateful for, so I decided to be grateful for everything. I didn't feel grateful. I willed it. I made myself think grateful thoughts.

When I thought about the layers of peeling wallpaper, I thanked God. I thanked God for each thing I hated about that house. I thanked Him for giving it to me. I thanked Him I was there. I even thanked Him I hated it. Each time I had a negative thought about the house, I countered it with a grateful one.

Maybe this wasn't as logical a reaction as negativity, but it turned out to be more effective. After I practiced gratitude for about three of four months, things started to change.

My attitude changed. I stopped sitting and crying in the middle of the floor and started to accept the house—as it was. I started taking care of the house as though it were a dream home. I acted as if it were my dream home. I kept it clean, orderly, as nice as could be.

Then, I started thinking. If I took all the old wallpaper off first, maybe the paint would stay on. I pulled up some of the orange carpeting and discovered solid oak floors throughout the house. I went through some boxes I had packed away and found antique lace curtains that fit the windows. I found a community action program *that sold decent wallpaper for a dollar a roll. I learned about textured paint, the kind that fills and covers old, cracked walls. I decided if I didn't know how to do the work, I could learn. My mother volunteered to help me with wallpapering. Everything I needed came to me.*

Nine months later, I had a beautiful home. Solid oak floors glistened throughout the house. Country-print wallpaper and textured white walls contrasted beautifully with the dark, scrolled woodwork that decorated each room.

Whenever I encountered a problem — half the cupboard doors are missing and I don't have money to hire a carpenter — I willed gratitude. Pretty soon, a solution appeared: tear all the doors off and have an open, country kitchen pantry.

I worked and worked, and I had three floors of beautiful home. It wasn't perfect, but it was mine and I was happy to be there. Proud to be there. Truly grateful to be there. I loved that home.

Soon the house filled up with furniture too. I learned to selectively collect pieces here and there for $5 and $10, cover the flaws with lace doilies, and refinish. I learned how to make something out of almost nothing, instead of nothing out of something.

I have had the opportunity to practice the gratitude principle many times in my recovery. It hasn't failed me. Either I change, my circumstances change, or both change.

"But you don't know how deprived I am!" people say. "You don't know everything I've gone without. You don't know how difficult it is right now. You don't know what it's like to have nothing!"

Yes, I do. And gratitude is the solution. Being grateful for what we have today doesn't mean we have to have that forever. It means we acknowledge that what we have today is what we're supposed to have today. There is enough, we're enough, and all we need will come to us. We don't have to be desperate, fearful, jealous, resentful, or miserly. We don't have to worry about what someone else has; they don't have ours. All we need to do is appreciate and take care of what we have today. The trick is, we need to be grateful first—before we get anything else, not afterward.

Then, we need to believe that we deserve the best life has to offer. If we don't believe that, we need to change what we believe we deserve. Changing our beliefs about what we deserve isn't an overnight process. Whether we're talking about relationships, work, home, or money, this usually happens in increments. We believe we deserve something a little better, then a little better, and so on. We need to start where we're at, changing our beliefs as we're capable. Sometimes things take time.

Believing we deserve good things is as important as gratitude. Practicing gratitude without changing what we believe we deserve may keep us stuck in deprivation.

"I earned $30,000 a year and every morning I got into my ten-year-old car with a busted heater and thanked God for it. I was so grateful," says one woman who's recovering from codependency. "My kids would encourage me to buy a new car and I'd say no; I was just grateful to have my old one. Then one day, when I was talking to someone about deprivation, it hit me that I could afford to have a new car if I really believed I deserved one. I changed my mind about what I deserved, then went out and bought a new car."

There are times in our lives when depriving ourselves helps build character, renders us fit for certain purposes, or is part of "paying our dues" as we stretch toward goals. There is a purpose as well as a beginning and an end to the deprivation. Many of us have carried this too far. Our deprivation is without purpose or end.

In an Andy Capp cartoon strip, Andy's wife came to him one day grumbling about her tattered coat. "That coat of mine is a disgrace. I'm ashamed to go out in it. I'll really have to get a new one," she said.

"We'll see, we'll see," he replied.

"Roughly translated," she said, scrunching up her face, "you never know what you can do without until you try."

Well, we never know what we can have until we try. And we may not know what we already have until we get grateful. Be grateful and believe you deserve the best. You may have more today than you think. And tomorrow might be better than you can imagine.

Beyond Codependence, Beattie, Melody; Hazelden Foundation: Center City, MN, 1989

PATTERNS AND CHARACTERISTICS OF CODEPENDENCE [9]

These patterns and characteristics are offered as a tool to aid in self-evaluation. They may be particularly helpful to newcomers.

Denial Patterns:

- I have difficulty identifying what I am feeling.
- I minimize, alter or deny how I truly feel.
- I perceive myself as completely unselfish and dedicated to the well being of others.

Low Self Esteem Patterns:

- I have difficulty making decisions.
- I judge everything I think, say or do harshly, as never "good enough."
- I am embarrassed to receive recognition and praise or gifts.
- I do not ask others to meet my needs or desires.
- I value others' approval of my thinking, feelings and behavior over my own.
- I do not perceive myself as a lovable or worthwhile person.

Compliance Patterns:

- I compromise my own values and integrity to avoid rejection or others' anger.
- I am very sensitive to how others are feeling and feel the same.
- I am extremely loyal, remaining in harmful situations too long.
- I value others' opinions and feelings more than my own and am afraid to express differing opinions and feelings of my own.
- I put aside my own interests and hobbies in order to do what others want.
- I accept sex when I want love.

Control Patterns:

- I believe most other people are incapable of taking care of themselves.
- I attempt to convince others of what they "should" think and how they "truly" feel.
- I become resentful when others will not let me help them.
- I freely offer others advice and directions without being asked.
- I lavish gifts and favors on those I care about.
- I use sex to gain approval and acceptance.
- I have to be "needed" in order to have a relationship with others.

THE TWELVE STEPS OF CO-DEPENDENTS ANONYMOUS [10]

1. *We admitted we were powerless over others – that our lives had become unmanageable.*

2. *Came to believe that a power greater than ourselves could restore us to sanity.*

3. *Made a decision to turn our will and lives over to the care of God as we understood God.*

4. *Made a searching and fearless moral inventory of ourselves.*

5. *Admitted to God, to ourselves, and to another human being, the exact nature of our wrongs.*

6. *Were entirely ready to have God remove all these defects of character.*

7. *Humbly asked God to remove our shortcomings.*

8. *Made a list of all persons we had harmed and became willing to make amends to them all.*

9. *Made direct amends to such people wherever possible, except when to do so would injure them or others.*

10. *Continued to take personal inventory and when we were wrong, promptly admitted it.*

11. *Sought through prayer and meditation to improve our conscious contact with God as we understood God, praying only for knowledge of God's will for us and the power to carry that out.*

12. *Having had a spiritual awakening as the result of these steps, we tried to carry this message to other codependents, and to practice these principles in all our affairs.*

Support

To reach Co-Dependents Anonymous, Inc. (CoDA) please contact:

Web: www.coda.org

Mail: CoDA, Fellowship Services Office, PO Box 33577, Phoenix, AZ 85067-3577

Phone (answering service only): (888) 444-2359 (Toll free) or (602) 277-7991 (Meeting information only)

Email: outreach@coda.org (Outreach answers general questions concerning CoDA and can help get you into contact with the right committee.)

PATTERNS AND CHARACTERISTICS OF CODEPENDENCE and THE TWELVE STEPS OF CO-DEPENDENTS ANONYMOUS are reprinted from the website www.CoDA.org with permission of Co-Dependents Anonymous, Inc. (CoDA). Permission to reprint this material does not mean that CoDA has reviewed or approved the contents of this book, or that CoDA agrees with the views expressed herein. CoDA is a fellowship of men and women whose common purpose is to develop healthy relationships and is not affiliated with any other 12 step program.

Addiction

CHILDREN OF ADDICTED PARENTS: IMPORTANT FACTS [11]

Alcoholism and other drug addiction tend to run in families. Children of addicted parents are more at risk for alcoholism and other drug abuse than are other children.

- Children of addicted parents are the group of children most at risk of becoming alcohol and drug abusers due to both genetic and family environment factors.
- Children with a biological parent who is alcoholic continue to have an increased risk (2-9 fold) of developing alcoholism even when they have been adopted. This fact supports the hypothesis that there is a genetic component in alcoholism.
- Recent studies further suggest a strong genetic component, particularly for early onset of alcoholism in males. Sons of alcoholic fathers are at fourfold risk (of future substance abuse) compared with the male offspring of non-alcoholic fathers.
- Use of substances by parents and their adolescent children is strongly correlated; generally, if parents take drugs, sooner or later their children will also. Adolescents who use drugs are more likely than their non-addicted peers to have one or more parents who also use drugs.
- The influence of parental attitudes on a child's drug-taking behaviors may be as important as actual drug abuse by the parents. An adolescent who perceives that a parent is permissive about the use of drugs is more likely to use drugs.

Family interaction is defined by substance abuse or addiction in a family.

- *Families affected by alcoholism report higher levels of conflict than do families with no alcoholism. Drinking is the primary factor in family disruption. The environment of children of alcoholics has been characterized by lack of parenting, poor home management, and lack of family communication skills, thereby effectively robbing children of alcoholic parents of modeling or training in parenting skills or family effectiveness.*

- *The following family problems have frequently been associated with families affected by alcoholism: increased family conflict; emotional or physical violence; decreased family cohesion; decreased family organization; increased family isolation; increased family stress including work problems, illness, marital strain and financial problems; and frequent family moves.*

- *Addicted parents often lack the ability to provide structure or discipline in family life, but simultaneously expect their children to be competent at a wide variety of tasks earlier than do non-addicted parents.*

- *Sons of addicted fathers are the recipients of more detrimental discipline practices from their parents.*

A relationship between parental addiction and child abuse is indicated in a large proportion of child abuse and neglect cases.

- *Three of four (71.6%) child welfare professionals cite substance abuse as the chief cause for the dramatic rise in child maltreatment since 1986.*

- *Most welfare professionals (79.6%) report that substance abuse causes or contributes to at least half of all cases of child maltreatment; 39.7% say it is a factor in over 75% of the cases.*

- *In a sample of parents who significantly maltreat their children, alcohol abuse specifically is associated with physical maltreatment, while cocaine abuse exhibits a specific relationship to sexual maltreatment.*

- *Children exposed prenatally to illicit drugs are 2 to 3 times more likely to be abused or neglected.*

Children of drug addicted parents are at greater risk for placement outside the home.

- *Three of four child welfare professionals (75.7%) say that children of addicted parents are more likely to enter foster care, and 73% say that children of alcoholics stay longer in foster care than do other children.*

- *In one study, 79% of adolescent runaways and homeless youth reported* alcohol use in the home, 53% reported problem drinking in the home, and 54% reported drug use in the home.

- *Each year, approximately 11,900 infants are abandoned at birth or are kept at hospitals, 78% of whom are drug-exposed. The average daily cost for each of these babies is $460.*

Children of addicted parents exhibit symptoms of depression and anxiety more than do children from non-addicted families.

- *Children of addicted parents exhibit depression and depressive symptoms more frequently than do children from non-addicted families.*

- *Children of addicted parents are more likely to have anxiety disorders or to show anxiety symptoms.*

- *Children of addicted parents are at high risk for elevated rates of psychiatric and psychosocial dysfunction, as well as for alcoholism.*

Children of addicted parents experience greater physical and mental health problems and generate higher health and welfare costs than do children from non-addicted families.

- *Inpatient admission rates and average lengths of stay for children of alcoholics are 25-30% greater than for children of non-alcoholic parents. Substance abuse and other mental disorders are the most notable conditions among children of addiction.*

- *It is estimated that parental substance abuse and addiction are the chief cause in 70-90% of all child welfare spending. Using the more conservative 70% assessment, in 1998 substance abuse and addiction accounted for approximately $10 billion in federal, state and local government spending simply to maintain child welfare systems.*

- *The economic costs associated with Fetal Alcohol Syndrome were estimated at $1.9 billion for 1992.*

- *A sample of children hospitalized for psychiatric disorders demonstrated that more than 50% were children of addicted parents.*

Children of addicted parents have a higher-than-average rate of behavior problems.

- *One study comparing children of alcoholics (aged 6-17 years) with children of psychiatrically healthy medical patients, found that children of alcoholics had elevated rates of ADHD (Attention Deficit Hyperactivity Disorder) and ODD (Oppositional Defiant Disorder) compared to the control group of children.*

- • *Research on behavioral problems demonstrated by children of alcoholics has revealed some of the following traits: lack of empathy for other persons, decreased social adequacy and interpersonal adaptability, low self-esteem, and lack of control over the environment.*

- • *Research has shown that children of addicted parents demonstrate behavioral characteristics and a temperament style that predispose them to future maladjustment.*

Children of addicted parents score lower on tests measuring school achievement and exhibit other difficulties in school.

- *Sons of addicted parents performed worse on all domains measuring school achievement, using the Peabody Individual Achievement Test-Revised (PIAT-R), including general information, reading recognition, reading comprehension, total reading, mathematics and spelling.*

- *In general, children of alcoholic parents do less well on academic measures. They also have higher rates of school absenteeism and are more likely to leave school, be retained, or be referred to the school psychologist than are children of non-alcoholic parents.*

- *In one study, 41% of addicted parents reported that at least one of their children repeated a grade in school, 19% were involved in truancy, and 30% had been suspended from school.*

- *Children of addicted parents were found at significant disadvantage on standard scores of arithmetic compared to children of non-addicted parents.*

- *Children of alcoholic parents often believe that they will be failures even if they do well academically. They often do not view themselves as successful.*

Children of addicted parents score lower on tests measuring verbal ability.

- *Children of addicted parents tend to score lower on tests that measure cognitive and verbal skills. Their ability to express themselves may be impaired, which can hamper their school performance, peer relationships, ability to develop and sustain intimate relationships, and performance on job interviews.*

- *Lower verbal scores, however, should not imply that children of addicted parents are intellectually impaired.*

Children of addicted parents have greater difficulty with abstraction and conceptual reasoning.

- *Abstraction and conceptual reasoning play an important role in problem solving, whether the problems are academic or are related to situations encountered in life. Children of alcoholics may require very concrete explanations and instructions.*

Maternal consumption of alcohol and other drugs any time during pregnancy can cause birth defects or neurological deficits.

- *Studies have shown that exposure to cocaine during fetal development may lead to subtle but significant deficits later on, especially with skills that are crucial to success in the classroom, such as the ability to block distractions and concentrate for long periods.*

- *Cognitive performance is less affected by alcohol exposure in infants and children whose mothers stopped drinking in early pregnancy, despite the mothers' resumption of alcohol use after giving birth.*

- *Prenatal alcohol effects have been detected at moderate levels of alcohol consumption in nonalcoholic women. Even though a mother may not regularly abuse alcohol, her child may not be spared the effects of prenatal alcohol exposure.*

Children of addicted parents may benefit from supportive adult efforts to help them.

- *Children who coped effectively with the trauma of growing up in families affected by alcoholism often relied on the support of a non-alcoholic parent, stepparent, grandparent, teachers and others.*

- *Children in families affected by addiction who can rely on other supportive adults have greater autonomy and independence, stronger social skills, better ability to cope with difficult emotional experiences, and better day-to-day coping strategies than other children of addicted parents.*

- *Group programs reduce feelings of isolation, shame and guilt among children of alcoholics while capitalizing on the importance to adolescents of peer influence and mutual support.*

- *Competencies such as the ability to establish and maintain intimate relationships, express feelings, and solve problems can be improved by building the self-esteem and self-efficacy of children of alcoholics.*

Support

For more information contact:

National Association for Children of Alcoholics
11426 Rockville Pike, Suite 301
Rockville, Maryland 20852

Phone: 888-55-4COAS or 301-468-0985

Fax: 301-468-0987

E-mail: nacoa@nacoa.org

Web: www.nacoa.net

Source: The National Association for Children of Alcoholics (NACoA)

Bibliography

1. *Tammy* – Music by Jay Livingston, lyrics by Ray Evans. Published in 1957 and released by Coral Records, catalog number 61851.

2. *Go Your Own Way* – Music and lyrics by Lindsey Buckingham. Published in 1976 and released by Warner Bros.

3. *How Great Thou Art* – Christian hymn based on a Swedish poem written by Carl Gustav Boberg (1859–1940) in Sweden in 1885. Translated into English by British missionary Stuart K. Hine in 1949.

4. *Cherish* – Music and lyrics by Terry Kirkman. Published in 1966 and released by Valiant Records.

5. *Boundaries: When to Say Yes, When to Say No to Take Control of Your Life*, Cloud, Henry and Townsend, John; Zondervan: Grand Rapids, MI, April 1992.

6. *Domestic Violence Facts*, National Coalition Against Domestic Violence; Washington, DC, Copyright © 2005-2009. All Rights Reserved.

7. *Co-Dependent No More*, Beattie, Melody; Hazelden Foundation: Center City, MN, 1986, 1992.

8. *Beyond Codependence*, Beattie, Melody; Hazelden Foundation: Center City, MN, 1989.

9. *Patterns and Characteristics of Codependence*, Co-Dependents Anonymous, Inc.; Phoenix, AZ, Copyright © 1998. All Rights Reserved.

10. *The Twelve Steps of Co-Dependents Anonymous*, Co-Dependents Anonymous, Inc.; Phoenix, AZ, Copyright © 1998. All Rights Reserved.

11. *Children of Addicted Parents: Important Facts – A Kit for Educators*, Fourth Edition, National Association for Children of Alcoholics; Rockville, MD, Copyright © 2001.